DOVE DESCENDING

A Journey into T. S. Eliot's *Four Quartets*

THOMAS HOWARD

DOVE DESCENDING

A Journey into T. S. Eliot's *Four Quartets*

SAPIENTIA CLASSICS

IGNATIUS PRESS   SAN FRANCISCO

Cover image: © Royalty-Free / Corbis
Cover design by Riz Boncan Marsella

© 2006 Ignatius Press, San Francisco
All rights reserved
ISBN 978-1-58617-040-0
ISBN 1-58617-040-6
Library of Congress Control Number 2005933380

Printed in the United States of America ∞

CONTENTS

FOREWORD

T. S. Eliot was the quintessential modern poet by being the last modern poet. The ability to speak of the modern in the past tense exposes a nervous tension in the concept of the modern as "the only now". Modernity's isolation from time past and future evaporated anthropological radicalism by its superficiality and made banality an enterprise. I am aware of no other age that was so self-conscious: the Greeks did not think of themselves as classical, nor did the Scholastics think of themselves as highly medieval. But modern people justified everything they did by calling it modern. The end of the modern age was not like the end of any other age, for the essence of modernity was that it was not supposed to end: and so while other ages contribute their echoes to the development of culture, the modern age erased itself by succumbing to the future. Like John the Baptist, who was the greatest of the prophets by being the last of them, so was Eliot the most blatant voice of modernism by ending it when he wrote the *Four Quartets*. What comes next is yet to be grasped, but the vague and properly vacuous term "postmodern" means that the only substance of modernity, its unsurpassibility, was a phantom.

The blood and bones of Eliot spanned the modern age. On the day of his birth, the newspapers carried the latest news of Jack the Ripper; and the day he died, Lyndon Johnson proposed his "Great Society". Edison invented the kinetoscope as Eliot was born; and Penzias and Wilson confirmed the "Big Bang" theory with their evidence of cosmic microwave background radiation as Eliot's ashes were being sent to East Coker. It is as if he were finally providing a footnote to his lines by means of his own biology: "What we call the beginning is often the end. And to make an end is to make a beginning. The end is where we start from." The exhaustion of living through modern changes, like any exhaustion, is the ground of depression. Thus the dolours of *The Waste Land*. But if the end is where we start from, there is a cure in the permanent Augustinian metaphysic that is not intimidated by chronology. The *Four Quartets* are a hymn of confidence.

Even in our litigious age it is difficult to sue universities for philosophical malpractice. Much as I revere the dappled lawns of my New England college days, I have a case against some of my teachers, for they made me wallow through *The Waste Land* with no mention of "Burnt Norton" or "East Coker" or "The Dry Salvages" or, the Ultimate Concern forefend, "Little Gidding". What they taught about Eliot was equivalent to saying that Saul of Tarsus was a driven man who had roughed up the first Christians, without mentioning his Damascus Road and consequent epistles. The impression was that Eliot had been cut from the same cloth as the chic French existentialists. When my French professor, who idolized Sartre, put his head in a gas oven, it would not have surprised me if Eliot were next. Instead, Eliot died a natural death just a few months before I graduated. By then I knew that he had a different view of things. It was almost forensically that one read in his obituary in *The Times* how "few . . . saw through the surface innovations and the language of despair to the deep respect for tradition and keen moral sense which underlay them." Reading those courteous lines now, after having read what Thomas Howard writes about the real Eliot, my gums dry and my eyes burn at the enormous condescension of those well-meaning funereal words written in 1965. Having a deep respect for tradition is like saluting an earthquake, and a keen moral sense sounds like the happiness that comes from good dental hygiene.

The *Four Quartets*, like the *Odyssey* and I suppose every poem, really, are meant to be heard. It may be carried to eccentric lengths, like the recordings of Dame Edith Sitwell (who, bless her, went to a length in religion greater than retentive Eliot), but it is a fact: Why write in meters if the meters are not to be sung? I tried once, unsuccessfully, to persuade some rap singers on my Manhattan street corner that they were singing the same rhythms that Homer sent around Iona. (You could stretch this and say something similar about the opening tetrameters in section II of "Burnt Norton".) But I think I was correct. The first time I heard the *Quartets* read publicly was by a favorite actress, Prunella Scales, in the University Church of St. Mary the Virgin in Oxford on the centenary of Eliot's birth. She said that her son's headmaster coached her Greek pronunciation. I was entranced by her, as I had been when she played Miss Mapp and Mrs. Fawlty, but I confess that this seemed the only time her script bored me. I am indebted to Professor Howard for his advice on how to hear Eliot's lines, not in a deconstructionist way (Eliot's objective epistemology saved him from being a proto-Derrida, who is now decomposing in contradiction of his own theories), but as one hears music. Similarly, the philosopher Elizabeth Anscombe, who was ever patient with my student mind, insisted that Wittgenstein wanted his philosophical texts read as poetry and disdained classical philosophical syntax. At least in terms of shock value, Eliot was brother to Wittgenstein. I am grateful to Thomas Howard also for solving the puzzle of why these vivid quintets are called quartets, when the sections have a dangling fifth part. It has nothing to do with the scheme, and every-

thing to do with the voices. There are four instruments.
Now, Howard proposes along with others that these are the
primeval elements of air, earth, water, fire. It is a good argu-
ment, and it cannot be called a critic's conceit, but his grace-
ful analysis whetted my appetite. Eliot's concluding cache in
"Little Gidding" from Dame Julian's "Shewings" made me
go back to her original lines, as she is ventriloquist for the
Almighty God of Grace: "I may make all things well, and I
can make all things well, and I shall make all things well, and
I will make all things well, and thou shalt see thyself that
all manner of things shall be well." Dame Julian wrote that
on her sickbed in the Black Death; Eliot wrote that in 1942
during the world's blackest war. These tenses—*may . . . can
. . . shall . . . will*—thawing the frozen "only now" tense of
the moderns, parallel the four metaphysical realities: what
may be done invokes the possibilities of time; what can be
done opens the mind to eternity; what shall be done points to
undeniable mortality; and what will be done is the benign
calculus of faith. The promise "thou shalt" is the final fifth:
the act of the will, which makes man a moral actor in the
drama of providence.

If I am obliged to write a foreword, I shall be forward
enough to say that I was never drawn to Eliot. He does not
thrill like Yeats. I knew some who knew him well and who
invariably venerated him, although they were usually of an
insecure academic sort that snobbishly dismissed his devoted
and long-suffering second wife. While Eliot was to me like
the seventeenth-century Dr. Fell of whom it was said, "I do
not like thee", in a Christian sense I still find much in him to
love while not confusing this bond of charity with a chain of
affinity. For one thing, there was an aura of pedantry about
him, whether in the footnotes of *The Waste Land* or in the
language pyrotechnics of *Four Quartets*. The generous soul of

Thomas Howard assumes that Eliot was as facile with Attic Greek and High German as he implied. Perhaps he was. Eliot's citations are too precise and buttoned. This does not discredit him. His purpose was valiant. Eliot as poet and Waugh as novelist embarked on much the same Christian adventure, just a generation after Belloc and Chesterton, and Eliot was not the misanthrope that blessed Waugh was. All of them, save Waugh to his credit, shared the same ethereal confusions about economics. Eliot was fascinated with Chesterton and said that he "did more than any man of his time" to "maintain the existence of the [Christian] minority in the world". He wrote that eulogy the year he published "Burnt Norton", and, for all its piety, one senses a slight reserve like that of *The Times'* tribute to himself. Eliot was more English than the English, and so I suspect that privately he found Chesterton hearty, which in Eliot's fixed Anglo-Saxon vision would not have been a compliment. And Chesterton was a romantic, certainly in his rotund un-Prufrockean verse, by his own boasting all bangs and no whimpers. *Four Quartets* and *The Ballad of the White Horse* obliquely hymn the same God, but one suspects that the *Ballad* gave Eliot heartburn. In turn, Chesterton would have found Eliot too precious for his pub crawls and rolling English roads, and he misread Prufrock because of that. Parenthetically, I believe that Robert Frost actually wrote the definitive New England poem "The Road Not Taken" in Chesterton's Olde England village of Beaconsfield. So the strands weave together and unweave, and, because I am not Penelope, I cannot explain it all, but we are dealing with good hearts trying to make sense of the existence of the human heart in a disheartened world. In *Four Quartets*, Eliot comes to the modernist's lattice window like the lover in the Song of Solomon, furtively chanting a benign proposal of which all this world's lights and shadows are intimations, and in his precise and occasionally affected diction he witnesses to the Doctors of the Church in this: the intellect is supernaturally perfected by the light of glory.

"The end is where we start from." Professor Howard calculates this to the time matrix of the Holy Mass, where the altar becomes the locus of the Catholic eternal now and confounds the isolated modern illusion of the only now. What is not sacramental is pathological, and the Eucharist is remedy for the social pathology that darkened the promise of Eliot's age. Eliot ends with Dante's rose and Dame Julian's revelation, in a domesticated kind of piety which ungirdles itself to bow before beatitude. Had Eliot lived longer, he might have come to the point where, domestic reserve abandoned and ecclesiastical provincialism thwarted, he might have acknowledged that an earlier poet named Gregory the Great was also the Vicar of Christ. Pope Gregory anathematized those who say that the blessed ones do not see God but only a light coming from him. In the social disintegration and moral trauma attendant upon the fall of modernity, Eliot paraphrased it in coruscating ways and radiant rays of words. A poet has no apostolic authority, and his prophecy is by intuition and sensibility to tradition; but when he is true to the truth, aesthetics burnishes his metaphysics and gives him the mantle of an evangelist.

George William Rutler
New York City

PREFACE

There is something daunting, not to say presumptuous, about embarking on any commentary on T. S. Eliot, or on any of his works. The whole thing has been done—and done, and done, a reader might justly murmur to himself. The shelf of Eliot studies would stretch from Tierra del Fuego to Ultima Thule, surely. The students, critics, scholars, and biographers who have addressed themselves to Elioteana, so to speak, constitute a dazzling galaxy. Is anyone calling for yet another meteorite to dash briefly across the firmament?

Probably not, or at least not in so many words. But the present volume makes only the most diffident claims for itself. It certainly does not belong to the genre "scholarship" or even "criticism". What I have attempted here is commonly known as "a reading". Over many years of having taught Eliot's poetry, I have found that people tend to run aground on his *Four Quartets*. Someone will, again justly, cry out, "Run aground on *Four Quartets*! What about all the rest of his sybilline poetry?" We all feel about Eliot's poetry the way W. H. Auden says he felt when he first tried to read the verse of Charles Williams: he "couldn't make head or tail of it". When the reading public, early in the twentieth century, called loudly for some footnote help on "The Waste Land", Eliot obliged by furnishing a set of notes even more cryptic than the poem itself. Even his short verse—"A Cooking Egg"—has us scratching our heads. We can't even get beyond the title. Is this an egg *for* cooking? Or is it an egg *that is* cooking?

During my own doctoral studies at New York University, I sat in my carrel in the library with great heaps of secondary works on Eliot all over the desk and the old green Harcourt Brace hardback *The Complete Poems and Plays* open in front of me, spiral notebook next to it. I annotated my copy until the margins were black with pencil jottings. I explicated every line of every poem from every critic's point of view.

This was helpful. At least it got one into the poetry. Eliot, however, in his very own Olympian way, would have cordially disapproved of the enterprise. I think he thought that this sort of effort was gilding the lily. On the other hand, he himself maintained that modern poetry *has* to be "difficult", since traditional poetic language has, alas, slipped almost wholly into cliché, and the poets have got to fight their way out of the morass. It's no use (he would have urged) telling us, "The sun that brief December day / Rose cheerless over hills of grey", and so forth. This will only lull us into a stupor deeper even than the one in which we all already snore. If poetry has to do with "purifying the dialect of the tribe" (more on this anon), then the poets are going to have to use some harsh astringents in order to bring about this purifying. Language, like water, goes stagnant if it does not move. Or, to change the metaphor (a tactic Eliot probably *would* have approved of, since his poetry is often a kaleidoscopic sequence of differing metaphors), language gets encrusted, and the poets have to come at the barnacles with hatchets.

Well. Back to *Four Quartets*. In my own view, this sequence of four poems—or this one single poem: it is not easy to settle even this elementary question—represents the pinnacle of Eliot's whole work. He worked on it (them?) over a period of several years in the late 1930s and early 1940s, after a long period of having produced a number of dramas. The work (let us settle for the singular, without arguing the point too shrilly) lies on the hither side of a Himalayan watershed from the early poetry that had made him the giant of English poetry in the twentieth century: Eliot had converted to orthodox Christian belief several years before he embarked on *Four Quartets*.

This conversion did not please Eliot's readers. He had been extolled as the voice of modernism, since he had put into mordantly succinct language the jumble of emotions held to be the very cockade of modernity: ennui, disenchantment, impotence, futility, vacuity, fatuity. His J. Alfred Prufrock would certainly be a front-running candidate for the post of Most Miserable Figure ever to appear on the pages of English literature. (Kafka's Gregor Samsa, who turned into a cockroach, might run Prufrock some competition, but of course he was *mitteleuropaisch*.) Old Prufrock is our hero, if by "our" we mean us mortals who find ourselves inhabiting a world from which meaning has vanished in the wake of—of what? Or whom? Descartes? Well, yes, certainly Descartes. But Hume and Kant and Darwin and Marx and Freud and a whole senate of others, including Picasso and Georges Braque, would all be in that boat leaving the unhappy wake behind its progress. Queen Victoria had died in 1901 and with her (so goes the story) an entire eon of moral certitude and rectitude and most of the canons of civility, reticence, decorum, and gentility that had been more or less in place in the West until then. World War I was dealing the coup de grace to everything anyway, so what was there left to do but either eat, drink, and be merry or "spit out all the butt-ends of my days" ("Prufrock", in *T. S. Eliot: The Complete Poems and Plays, 1909–1950*; New York: Harcourt, Brace, and World, 1952, p. 5). The story has been told ten thousand times over. What it comes to, I would venture to put forward at the risk of wild oversimplification, is the loss of God. Nietszche would agree with me, I think. Eliot came to this view with his conversion, certainly.

Four Quartets stands as Eliot's valedictory to the modern world. I myself would place it, along with Chartres Cathedral, the *Divine Comedy*, van Eyck's "Adoration of the Mystic Lamb", and the Mozart Requiem, as a major edifice in the history of the Christian West.

In the following "reading" of this work, I have pursued a strategy that I have found to be greatly helpful to students and other would-be readers of the poem. I teach from a thin copy that contains the *Four Quartets* and nothing else (New York: Harcourt, Brace, Jovanovich, 1971; all quotations hereafter are from this edition). I have numbered the lines in my own copy so that I can find things; but besides those numbers, there is scarcely a mark in the whole volume. The point here is that once one gets "on" to Eliot's own poetic strategy, one finds that footnotes are, to an overwhelming degree, adventitious. For example, we come to a garden. "Which garden is this?" cry all the students. "Eden? The Gardens of the Hesperides? The Hanging Gardens of Babylon? The medieval garden of *amour courtois*? My own tomato patch? What?" And Eliot would reply, "Whatever you like. A garden is a garden is a garden, is it not? Is not *any* garden a plot of land, designed and disciplined and cultivated in the interest of beauty and order, as opposed to a mere chaos of weeds or a junkyard?"

But with that last paragraph, I am anticipating myself. That is what this book is about. Of course, we have bumbled into a paradox before we start. If footnotes are adventitious, what is this whole book about, pray? A prickly question. My only rejoinder would run something like this: *Eliot* was not amiably disposed to the clutter that footnotes bring to poetry, which ought to be intelligible on its own terms. But there is the rub. A poet's language is a creation of his own and may have to be learned, just as French must be learned by English-speaking people. But introductory French-language textbooks are not filled with footnotes. They lead us along into the language, and, after having learned "*Le livre est sur la table*" (which is, I seem to recall, the first French sentence I learned as a small boy) and "*Je t'aime*", and so forth, presently we find that we are reading French and, it is to be hoped, speaking it, albeit for most English-speaking people, with execrable pronunciation.

My book, then, has almost no "scholarly" material in it. I may tell you that Little Gidding was a community founded by one Nicholas Ferrar in the seventeenth century in England, or I may fill in what Eliot apparently assumes we all should know, namely, what Krishna said to Arjuna. But beyond that, most of what I have to say is a prosaic, and terribly wooden (but necessary for newcomers to this difficult language?), rendering of what turns out to be infinitely more lucid, once it is understood, than all the talk with which we teachers scurry busily about the precincts.

PRELIMINARY REMARKS

Let us begin with the title. A quartet, in music, is a piece scored for four instruments, not necessarily a quartet in four movements. Eliot is drawing on this notion for his poem. What we have is a sequence of four poems with *five* sections in each. This confuses some beginning readers: What is this fifth movement doing in this *Quartet*? The answer is this: the four instruments are, probably, Air, Earth, Water, and Fire— the Four Elements that were assumed to be the major constituents of the material universe before the advent of modern science and its periodic chart of the atoms (and whatever it is that follows that: I last studied the matter in 1952 and know nothing of quarks, probabilities, singularities, and nanoseconds). Whatever Eliot knew of post-Einsteinean physics (he died in January 1965), he chose to draw upon this ancient ordering of things for the substance upon which to build his poem.

Burnt Norton, which furnishes the title to the first section of the *Quartets*, is the name of a seventeenth-century English manor house in Gloucestershire long since burned down. There is nothing left there but a spot of ground. We might think to ourselves, "Ah! So we begin with Earth." No. We will find that this section is shot through with the language of daylight, sunlight, *shafts* of sunlight, clouds, wind, darkness, the light glinting on a kingfisher's wing, and the stars, which are *up there*, if not in the air, then at least beyond the air, in space.

We may, at this point, observe that the titles for the four

sections of the poem each names a place. Burnt Norton—a house. East Coker—the village in Somerset to which Eliot traced his ancestry. The Dry Salvages—some rocks off Eastern Point in Gloucester, Massachusetts, which is where Eliot came as a boy with his parents to their summer house. (It may be noted here that Salvages is pronounced sal-*vay*-ges. I may also note that I live in the neighborhood and have many friends who sail, but no one has ever been able to tell me which set of rocks has that name. In fact, no one I know knows of any such rocks, although I daresay if I did some more assiduous inquiring in Gloucester, some fisherman would turn up whose grandfather had known about The Dry Salvages.) Little Gidding—the lay Anglican community referred to earlier, about which more when we come to it.

This is all crucial to Eliot's whole idea in the *Quartets*. If we can venture, at mortal risk, to attempt a *theme* for it all (readers will sigh, having heard that word too many times from their English teachers), we might say that it all has something to do with the odd business of being mortal, that is, intelligent creatures existing *here* and *in time*, when all the while we are profoundly dissatisfied with this dismal sequence of past, present, and future. Time, in other words. The trouble with time is that it drains things away. We mortals have "intimations of immortality" and wish things would stay put, but they don't. Houses burn down. Fields are bulldozed into highway interchanges ("bypasses", in British English). We die and are buried.

That, or something like that, is a good enough way for us to follow as we start our reading of the *Quartets*. Readers will work out their own statement of Eliot's theme after they have finished—except that my own experience has been that, far from wanting to boil the thing down to any statements, I would wish to say, "Theme? It takes every line in the whole work to enunciate the theme. You can't boil it down. If you could, then Eliot wasted his time working out these lines."

I *think* Eliot, and all serious poets (I am not one myself), would agree here. A poem is a thing. It is not a set of fancy trimmings to an otherwise obvious truth. Many readers suppose that that is exactly what poetry is: fancy trimmings. On the contrary, poetry is language brought to its most scorching, most succinct, most pellucid purity, like a Bunsen burner, where we want, not a bonfire, but a small prick of blue flame.

Burnt Norton

I

In the 1962 Harcourt, Brace, and World edition of *The Complete Poems and Plays, 1909–1950*, there is a subscript in Greek under the title "Burnt Norton". The translation would run like this: "Although Reason is common to all, most people live as though they had wisdom of their own." And, under that, another Greek statement: "The way up and the way down are one and the same."

Readers fret over Eliot's habit of treating us as though we all know as much as he did. It's all very well, we may complain, for you, Mr. Eliot, with your late nineteenth- and early twentieth-century education, which included Harvard and studies in Europe, to reach for the odd Greek, French, German, or *Langue d'oc* quotation, but we are a bit limited nowadays. In any event, those Greek fragments lie between the title and the first line of "Burnt Norton". Both reach deep into the entire work—all four of the *Quartets*: but we may say, sketchily, at the outset, that one of Eliot's concerns here is the paradox, lamentable to him, obviously, that we all have enough sense ("Reason") to know that Death will most certainly seal off everything that we have known so far of ourselves and the world, but that we do our best to sweep the baleful fact under the rug. Reason trumpets the fact to us; but we caper, or blunder, or dawdle, along as though we knew something *else* (some private wisdom of our own that notifies us of some exemption to doom). We will find in

"Burnt Norton" lines that will peel the veneer from this idiocy.

But what about this "way up" and "way down" being the same thing? Again, this is a needlelike paradox that pierces to the very center of the whole work. We will find, as we go along, that "the way"—that is, our movement through our mortal existence toward our "end" (in both senses of that word: our termination by death, and/or the fruition, or *telos*, for which we were made to begin with)—that that way is "up" in the sense of an ascent toward a higher destiny and "down" in the sense of the self-emptying that turns out to be, apparently, required of us if we are to reach that destiny. And let us be candid right here at the start: Eliot was a Christian believer, and this "destiny" was no vague universalist or Buddhist absorption into the Whole: it was the Beatific Vision— that is, the Vision of God. It may be apposite here, also, to remind readers that Eliot was profoundly "catholic" in his vision, albeit Anglican, not Roman. Hence, his vocabulary— e.g., the Beatific Vision—assumes the ordinary coinage of catholic discourse, piety, and vision. Non-religious, or Protestant, readers sometimes find Eliot's vocabulary in this connection a bit steep (as who does not find his vocabulary a bit steep anyway? "haruspicate" or "etiolated", forsooth).

We find in the first eight lines of "Burnt Norton" language that presents itself as flat prose (and anyone who has heard the recording of Eliot reading *Four Quartets* will know that that is exactly how he reads them). Here is no Byronic rolling on of deep and dark blue oceans or Shakespearean spouting of hurricanes. Just flat statement (apparently) about the extremely difficult topic of time. The idea that "Time present and time past / Are both perhaps present in time future" is not altogether strange, of course. Anyone who has ever scratched his head over the riddle of time will no doubt have fancied that perhaps the whole sequence rolls up, like yarn, into some Ultimate Ball. We don't like the notion of things simply fraying off into the ether. Might it not be (we venture) that the present and the past are not *nothing*? Or, Eliot continues, time future is perhaps contained in time past. That is, the ball of yarn (the metaphor is not a very good one and not Eliotean at all) might be back at the beginning, and time as we know it is the strand of yarn being pulled out into a long length, so that what *will be* (the future) is somehow already *there* at the beginning, designed, foreseen, or "in the cards", so to speak.

A thousand religious and philosophical efforts have been made to come at this puzzle. We cannot canvass them all here; so let us pick a case in point of what Eliot is speaking of, although he is not, by a long shot, speaking of this case in point *yet*. The Mass. Eliot was a faithful communicant at Mass. The notion at work in the Mass is that *that which* "was" eternally true (the Lamb of God "slain from the foundation of the world"), and which "will be" unveiled in the consummation of all things, namely, the eschatological appearance of the Mystic Lamb pictured in Saint John's Apocalypse, is *here—now—on this altar*. It may be ten o'clock on a Sunday morning at Saint Paul's Gloucester Road (Eliot's parish) in 1942: but all of eternity—"past", "present", and "future"—is here, both in time and in this place. Where are we—or, in what *when* are we—at Mass? We are with God in a past eternity when the Redemption of the world was hatched; and we are in Eden when animals' blood had to be spilled to clothe the guilty Adam and Eve; and we are in the Holy of Holies with Aaron with the blood of lambs; and we are at the Last Supper; and on Golgotha; and in the eschaton (heaven) before the Eternal Altar.

Here, then, would be a case in point of the oddity with

which we are hailed in the first lines of "Burnt Norton". The whole of the *Quartets* begins with this notion, or wish, if we will. We mortals cannot, or at least will not, settle for the bleak idea of time simply evaporating things. Our memory, if nothing else, won't leave things alone. It keeps presenting the past to us and plucking our sleeve with inconsolable yearning: oh, to be *back there* when everything was so tranquil, unstained, and blissful (says memory). And the present, here, now, in this perfect moment with my beloved, say, in the Cotswolds or the West Highlands or in some flower-sprinkled alpine meadow: tomorrow, alas, we must leave and return to the struggle and din of Heathrow and then home. Couldn't we just package this magic moment and keep it inviolate forever?

The next lines make this flat point: "If all time is eternally present / All time is unredeemable." Period. There's nothing we can do about it all if the only "reality" is this moment, and everything else (past and future) is illusion. Eliot raises the stakes here by introducing the word "redeem". He is obviously nudging us toward something more sober than mere nostalgia for the past or pipe-dreaming for the future. To redeem something is to *get it back*. A piece of property, say, or a prisoner. But time? How can we speak of redeeming time?

In the next few lines Eliot draws us toward a word that will turn out to be pivotal in his whole poem. "Point." As over against the melancholy notion of abstractions and mere possibilities, he introduces the idea that both what "might have been" and what actually "has been" *point* to an "end" that is always present. This *end* is not the dead end: it is the purpose, or the fruition, of things. And that fruition is always here—present. In this moment, here, now (Eliot repeats these words over and over), the whole meaning of things is gathered.

Everything that has been undergirds this moment, and everything that will be proceeds from it. And nothing is lost. Furthermore, all that has been, and even *what might have been*, "points" to this moment. That is, if we keep our wits about us we will be conscious of the oddity that time is not a mere tumble of shards, all cast higgledy-piggledy in a heap that we call "now". Rather, it constitutes a pattern that is unfolding. Take any pattern—the design on wallpaper, a gothic arch, a garden—and we will observe that all the parts both depend on all the other parts and also give meaning to all the other parts.

We have got only ten lines into the poem; but Eliot, with apparently extreme understatement (beware of Eliot's "understatements"), has already drawn us far into the vision of things upon which his poem proceeds and which his poem hopes to open up to us. From here on, he will be working these notions of time and memory for all they are worth.

With no break in the paragraph, we come upon this: "Footfalls echo in the memory / Down the passage which we did not take / Towards the door we never opened / Into the rose-garden." What is this? Alice in Wonderland? The passage which we did *not* take? The door we never opened? What rose-garden? Questions come clamoring.

Well, for one thing, of course, Eliot's very wording is haunting. Footfalls. Echo. That strange passage. That shut door. That garden. Eliot is mesmerizing us, surely?

He is. "My words echo / Thus, in your mind." I'm luring you along here, in spite of your resistance to being lured. (And, it will turn out, let it be said now, that Eliot is luring us toward solid, titanic, adamantine Reality. His poem is not a foxfire to entice us into a swamp.) He is about to probe this business of memory and nostalgia. Are they cues to something real? Or are they ingredients in an opiate?

But why ruffle up the dust on a bowl of rose-leaves? Eliot says he doesn't know. Other readers of this poem may loudly disagree with me here, but I think he jolly well does know. This "I do not know" is a tactic: a legitimate one, to be sure, since at this point he, being faithful to his little scenario here, as the persona in the drama, can't know. But this bowl of rose-leaves. Typical Eliot. We suddenly find ourselves with a wholly unlooked-for item in our laps. And we call for a footnote, please. But there is none. So what are we to do with this bowl? We are simply to recall what any bowl of rose-leaves *is*. Modern readers may not be familiar with potpourri, but our great-grandmothers often kept such things about. A nice silver or porcelain bowl sitting on a table, filled with the leaves of dried flowers—roses are the best flowers—giving off a faint and delicate fragrance. Dried flowers: the past, that is. These petals *used* to bloom. Now they are "dead": but their fragrance lingers into the present.

And not only that. They "are" *the past*, sitting here *in the present*. We may recall here Eliot's very prosaic opening lines about present, past, and future somehow being conflated, which is itself a line of thought that nudges us along toward the gigantic mystery addressed in the entirety of the *Quartets*. In the peculiarly astringent terms of poetry, Eliot is, of course, making a "raid" (more on this later in the poem) on the big questions that have bedeviled us mortals for eons: Where did we come from? What are we doing? Where are we going? The riddle of past, present, and future.

But this bowl of rose-leaves: Eliot's words "disturb" them. As long as they lie quietly there in their porcelain bowl on the table, all is manageable. We may have a pang of sadness as our gaze lights upon them before we sit down to chat. Or, if we get to thinking about them for very long, we may give way to tears. The past is gone—forever. Oh—those golden days, etc., etc. But Eliot will have no commerce with sentimentalism. His poetry is "dry". Modern poetry must be thus, he would urge, since the poetry of sentiment does nothing but cater to self-indulgence, and Eliot has something more taxing in mind.

So. "I do not know", says the voice in the poem. We haven't got anywhere near the outer precincts of any conceivable "answer" to the question as to why he should disturb the potpourri. But he does it anyway. Let's just stir these up here and see what happens.

Certainly memory is awakened. And now—"Other echoes". This business of "echoes": What about it? What *are* echoes? They are the illusionary response to some sound, returning to us, and seeming for all the world to be real ("Hey—there's my voice coming back across the lake from the mountainside!"). They are, in other words, an illusion that seems to restore to us something that has gone into the past (my voice, just two seconds ago).

By this time we are in a perilous realm: a garden full of echoes. The temptation to loiter, and perhaps sink into mere reverie, is strong. And the voice in the poem seems intent on intensifying that temptation. "Shall we follow?" It is a rhetorical question. There is only one answer: yes. Right. On we go—keeping our wits about us—wits, that is, that have been keeping pace with the poem. The *tone of the voice speaking* is the great antidote here to this temptation to sink into reverie, which, for Eliot, is a mere quagmire. Once again, he is not holding up an *ignis fatuus* for us, since such flickerings lead only into the mire. And Eliot's concern is Reality, not mire.

And now we have a bird—a thrush, we find out presently—calling us to be quick and "find them". Find *who*? Or *what*? Well, let us go through this gate: "Into our first world".

It would be a capricious reader who would insist here that this is anywhere but Eden. Call it what you want: Eden; Arcadia; the Golden Age; the primeval innocence. It is the idyllic state of affairs that lies at the root of all human imagination. All poetry, and all music, and all art, actually, testify to the inconsolable yearning in us to *recover* that state; or at least to glimpse it; or, at least as a *pis aller*, to mourn it. Even the roughest twentieth-century painting, music, and drama trumpet to us, "Something is wrong here! This can't be right!" But if there were no Eden (Carl Jung knew this), we would not know that we were exiles. Nostalgia would be an unknown frame of mind to us.

Eliot is undertaking a mortally dangerous task here. We are on the very edge of the mire—the useless mire of nostalgia. And his words seem to pile up on each other in the apparent attempt to lure us farther. Here's this thrush, and, if you know anything about ornithology, you know that the thrushes (robins, wood thrushes, and hermit thrushes) have perhaps the most beautiful songs of all. The notes of the hermit thrush deep in the spruce forest on an evening among the mountains will break your heart. And now we find this "them" whom the bird is hurrying us to find. Or, rather, we don't find them. We never *do* find them, actually. The closest we come to any actual "encounter" with them is a sharp sense that there are "presences" here. By this time, the demand that we must know, if you please, just who these presences *are* is hushed in everyone but the most churlish reader. Our whole attitude is one not only of extreme hesitancy, but of awe, and even of fear. Which is precisely the correct attitude for us in these precincts. Hold your questions, as Saint Peter was told to do at the Transfiguration, when he, like us here, found himself quite dreadfully out of his depth and tried to ameliorate things with chat. It won't do.

"They" turn out to be "dignified, invisible", and they, unlike us with the dried rose-leaves, do not disturb the dead leaves in the quivering ("vibrant") hot autumn air here. Any other aspect than dignity and invisibility would somehow diminish the mystery surrounding these presences. They are the presences, we must timorously concede, that do, in fact, people memory, especially remote memory—even our "racial memory" (Jung) of some long-lost idyll when all was well. (Aha: "well": keep that word in mind right through to the last five lines of the last of the *Quartets*.) We cannot approach those once-and-future (*quondam et futurus*, like Arthur's kingship) precincts more brashly than under this quivering and elusive mode of memory, furnished as it must be with garden, bird, unseen presences, and now "unheard music", forsooth.

The thirteen lines beginning with "And the bird called" draw us into the most highly charged and visionary intensity possible. Eliot, as always, is calmly in control. This is no séance, with the medium losing his moorings and flying off into some corybantic or dithyrambic frenzy. All of this "illusion" is in obedient, even pedestrian, service to the sheer truth of the matter, toward which Eliot patiently and ineluctably forges until the last line of the whole thing.

"Unheard music": What image will more exactly draw us to the thing that seems to lurk behind all music, right up to the most insupportable staves of the angelic Mozart? "Oh. *Oh!*" we want to cry as we hear these sounds. "What is it? Where does it come from? Of what unimaginable melody and harmony is this the adumbration?" These are questions that lacerate us, and Eliot, in two words, evokes this yearning of ours.

The business of "the unseen eyebeam" will perhaps need a genuine footnote for modern readers, since it does, in fact, allude to something that most of us have no way of knowing. In the Renaissance, and in seventeenth-century English poetry specifically, and in the poetry of John Donne most specifically, we come across the notion that, the eyes being the windows of the soul (this is smooth sailing so far, since this is a commonplace found even in the Bible), when two lovers gaze into each other's eyes, the "beams", so to speak, emanating from their eyes "cross", or even entwine. The image here captures for anyone who has ever loved the link with the beloved that the lover longs to gain. Here in this garden one would assume that *all* looks exchanged between those who are at home here would be marked by just this closely knit love. We (visitors) may be bemused by the notion: but the denizens of the garden know about it; and even we may, with the assistance of Eliot's lines, descry at a distance the bliss of that state of affairs from which we know ourselves to be exiles.

This may help us with the next, seemingly nonsensical, trope: What on earth might be this "look of flowers that are looked at"? Dear Eliot, we may want to cluck: you have gone too far now. No flower responds in the slightest way to being *looked at*. Come.

My own guess here is that this quality in the flowers partakes of the same ethos already introduced with the unheard music. All is aquiver here. All is intensity. All is peopled, and deep calleth unto deep. One deep (the perfect beauty of the rose) does, in fact, respond, like the seraphic antiphons of Paradise, to the mere business of being looked at. A rose *is* to be looked at. And, in the precincts of perfect joy, the rose, far from being inert, is itself "sensible". Perhaps "intelligent" would be going too far, but the notion of all sorts of echoes and antiphons flying and ringing among all *things* (not just of all *creatures*) seems to attend our efforts to come at the final nature of Joy. Indeed, to raise the stakes even higher, one might be pardoned for venturing that all things *are* in some sense "creatures", since they are Created (at least in Eliot's Christian view), and what is the noun that names something created? "Creature" would at least suggest itself. We, of course, from our post-Deist point of view, will harrumph, "Fie. Fie. Don't ask me to espouse some notion, straight from the realm of faerie, that *trees*, for example, or worse, *rocks*, are anything other than utterly inert and insensible."

Quite so. Or at least provisionally quite so. We can't get much response from trees and rocks, no matter how we hack at them. But the world on the hither side of the Sword that bars the gate to Eden is a massively silent world. We can no longer hear the Music of the Spheres, for example. And we have a difficult time with the psalmist when he calls upon frost and snow and wind to "Praise him and magnify him forever." But is there a state of affairs where indeed it may be said with more than mere fancy, Deep *calleth* unto deep? I suspect that Eliot would not scoff in this connection.

The picture here in the garden moves very quietly along. "There they were as our guests, accepted and accepting." Who is "they", and in what sense are they accepted and accepting? My own guess here is that they are the roses, and the dignified and invisible presences that now accompany us, having accepted the summons issued by our *memory* to appear on the scene. They, like us, now form part of the cast of characters. We move, naturally "in a formal pattern" (certainly we aren't scampering), "along the empty alley, into the box circle. . . ." By this time we readers, like those in the garden, are accepting. The empty alley? It's this alley that leads us along in this garden. Be it so. We will try to still our usual inclination to clamor for explanations.

This "box circle" is a very Eliotean item. Here in the

garden, it is obviously a hedge of boxwood planted and trimmed, creating a circular area. But any reader who has ever been to the opera knows that there is a box circle there as well—usually the tier of "boxes" where the bejewelled families sit, one level above the orchestra, or stalls, as Eliot would have called the ground-floor level of seats. Readers who know this, but who are new to Eliot, may wish to demand which circle he means here. And his reply, as always, would be, "Whichever you like. Both, probably." How so? Because both box circles are *cases in point* of something formal, designed, and beautiful, ordered to the solemnity that presides over the event (our visit to the garden or to the opera—or to our approach to whatever it is to which this odd vision serves as an aperture). The double meaning of this box circle is, in Eliot's view, of the very essence of poetry, since good poetry brings language to its purest intensity, under which any given word may open out in several directions. This was a characteristic that Eliot liked in the seventeenth-century English "metaphysical" poets. Their poetry is a logjam of meaning, although that is a misleading picture probably, since you are in trouble with a logjam, whereas the densely packed nature of metaphysical poetry leads toward lucidity and simplicity. A sardine tin might also come to mind here, as a case in point of something tightly packed in the interest of plenitude, but somehow sardine tins seem a bit rank in these precincts. Let us just say that density is a quality Eliot liked, and employed.

To revert to the phrase *case in point* for a moment: modern readers love to revel among symbols, since we all live in the backwash of Sigmund Freud. But what we find in the sudden and surprising arrival of odd items in Eliot's poetry is, in nearly every case, far more significant (dense, if we will) than a mere symbol. Symbols tend to be two-dimensional and not always organically of one piece with the thing they suggest. A hexagonal road sign equals "Stop". Fine. We all concur. Even metaphors, which stand much closer to the center of things than symbols, may be set aside once their import is clear. But a case in point of something is just that: a case in point. Eliot's friend Charles Williams seldom wrote about anything else. For him, your giving me a hand with my luggage is not a *symbol* of the Divine Charity. It is a case in point of that Charity, since, like the Cross, it exhibits, momentarily and infinitesimally, to be sure, exactly the same exchange, namely, "My life for yours". In the luggage situation, "my life" is merely a minute perhaps of inconvenience for you. Nevertheless, it is a real thing, and a fragment of your time is a real "piece" of your life, which you are donating for my assistance. The Cross, of course, is the ultimate case in point of the Divine Charity in our mortal history, and itself points to an eternal mystery, namely, the blissful exchanges of self-donation that obtain in the Most Holy Trinity.

We find ourselves looking down into a dry pool. Somebody, once upon a time, had the idea for this pool and had it excavated and made from concrete, probably for goldfish or whatever. All that is gone now, into the lost region of memory. But, in the vision into which we have been drawn, the pool fills with water. Very odd water it is, too: "water out of sunlight". But water doesn't come from sunlight, we protest (although let us hope that by now our protesting has modulated itself into hesitant wonder). Naturally there is a lotos floating on the surface. All lotoses have always spoken of the beauty, serenity, and fragrant repose of which they themselves are cases in point. "They" are behind us now—our dignified, invisible friends.

"Then a cloud passed." Clouds. What do they do—real, meteorological clouds? They darken and obscure things, and they change the ambience. They are not symbols. They really are up there, and they really do affect our inner being quite uncompromisingly. The vision has gone. Alas.

But no. Not alas. It turns out that the evaporating of the vision is a good thing. Our own wish to luxuriate in these tranquil precincts is understandable. Here the fever of life has been assuaged. But the bird says, "Go!" The same bird that lured us into this "unreality". His command coincides with our sudden awareness that the trees and shrubbery here are full of children, "hidden excitedly". Why doesn't Eliot have them *hiding*? Certainly children hide excitedly in all sorts of games. It may seem a quibble: but my own guess is that his choice of word here has to do with the *sound* of the line. "Hidden" flows more easily along than "hiding". Try it out loud. The long i and the –ing demand more of our sound-forming apparatus than the short i and the –en. Lest readers suppose that we have worked ourselves into an impossibly cramped corner with this sort of narrow scrutiny of a couple of sounds, they may be reminded that it is just this sort of thing that every good poet struggles with in every line he writes. It is as important as Mozart's choosing an E-flat instead of an E-natural at a given point. Everything that the poet or composer wants at this point stands or falls with just such minuscule considerations.

The "containing" here could refer either to the leaves or to the children. Probably Eliot would not object to either option. Nay, he has left his syntax this way because he believes in this sort of paradoxical ambiguity: ambiguity, because ambiguity is the very vessel of double (dense) meaning; and paradoxical, because ambiguity, which ordinarily blurs things here, in its proper poetic usage does the opposite. It clarifies, or intensifies. This laughter is "contained" in the leaves, or in the children. A lesser poet might have had the laughter "emanating" or some equally unsatisfactory state of affairs. But this laughter is contained: it is of one seamless fabric with the whole backdrop. It belongs to vision and not to the much woollier focus that marks our ordinary, and rather sloppy, way of glancing at things.

But why must we "Go, go, go"? The very bird that lured (remember "the deception of the thrush") us into this *un*real purlieu is suddenly getting peremptory. Go! Why?

Because "human kind / Cannot bear very much reality."

That line deserves a paragraph to itself in my page of prose here. We already know that that statement is true, but in a thousand years most of us would never have thought of it. We know, for example, that we cannot bear very much of the reality of flames. We need a hearth between us and the fire. Or water: in a glass or a pool or a lake or river, all is well (the lake and the river have banks, let us recall). But the ocean? The surf is great fun *if there is not too much of it.* If there is, we flee inland. And who will boast that he has anything but the most somber respect for the seascape of mid-ocean? Too much water here, and quite uncontrollable. Or sound: "That jackhammer is shattering my nerves!" "Turn that amplifier down!" Or art: "I've just spent two hours among these Giottos, and I cannot take any more." Why not? Too much illusion? (After all, it is only pigment on plaster—very manageable, one would have thought.) No. Too much reality. Or music: we totter away from *La Traviata* or the Mozart Requiem, regaled or thunderstruck as the case may be, but certainly unable to bear any more. Or sex: if an orgasm lasted much longer we would go mad. Or the vision of God, which is the ultimate Reality: I am not ready for it *at all* right now, thank you very much. What eons will be required to prepare me for this final Reality, God alone knows. But thank heaven that the heavens don't split open and allow us to gaze straight at the Sapphire Throne. Everyone in the Bible who found

himself facing a mere angel—only a messenger of the holy—
fell on his face in fright. Human kind, it seems, cannot bear
very much reality.

The *Four Quartets* exist(s) on the cusp between dim ordi-
nariness and the Eternal. Eliot, being mortal, is aware that to
lead us along this cusp is as daunting a task as the greatest poet
might ever ask for and that it will take unflagging poetic *tact*
to keep the enterprise on track. The danger, on the one
hand, is of our flying off into a merely esthetic ether and, on
the other, of our retreating to the "distractions" (more on this
later—much more) that commonly shield our attention from
Reality.

With no space after that line about how much reality we
can sustain, Eliot offers an observation very close to what he
gives us in line 1 of the whole work. Except that now we
have shifted, slightly, to "Time past and time future". But
again, with no punctuation at all following "future", we find
"What might have been and what has been". It is all one, as it
were. The echoing footfalls, the door we never opened, the
rose-garden, the bowl of rose-leaves, the vision: the might-
have-beens over which we yearn, and the brittle actuality
of what-has-been—all "Point to one end, which is always
present".

What "end"? Well, we haven't got there yet. But we should
by this time know this much: this "end" is the Greek *telos*
(fulfillment of destiny), or it is the dead end (death). Again
the ambiguity that illumines rather than blurs. Certainly, if all
time is unredeemable, then death will disclose nothing. But
if, as Eliot clearly hints in the opening lines, this may not be
the case, then death, the end, may boost us straight into the
telos, which pertains to our very humanity. Tact again: Eliot
will not rush ahead of himself. He is a poet, not a stump
preacher.

II

Where on earth are we now? "Garlic and sapphires in the mud"? Pray tell.

No two things could be more violently unlike each other than garlic and sapphires. And that is precisely what our quotidian existence is like: a great jumble of miscellany, all jostling and clashing, and no very apparent harmony at all. No relation of one thing to another. Swallowing an aspirin, deciding to declare war (if you are the president), sitting for an examination, hurrying through lunch, hurrying to a committee meeting, waiting in a traffic jam, coping with a heartbroken child, telephoning the plumber, finding oneself at Mass: my word! Who will orchestrate this clutter?

Garlic (the rank things, *or* the delicately spicy, depending on one's taste) and sapphires (the inexpressibly beautiful). The trouble is, the disarray in which one comes upon them makes this business of driving the chariot of my life through the mud of life mightily hard.

But before we go farther in this line-by-line crawl, we might take stock of the whole section that appears here under the Roman numeral II. It has to do with *pattern*. We have already, of course, come upon this notion with the box circle and the garden. And here we seem to blunder into the complete absence of pattern—all this garlic and so forth clotting the axle of my chariot. What we have here is a very Eliotean tactic. He does not very often *comment* on his poetry—or *in* his poetry, we might say. That is, he simply forges ahead, the way a sculptor knocks away bits of marble, as though to say, What is emerging here *is* the answer to your question as to what I am doing. I don't need to tell you "This is an arm" or "This is a toe." Just follow my work. Watch how I am shaping

my materials. It is thus with Eliot and his materials, which are
words, of course. So far we have had the problem of time and
its apparent irrecoverability raised for us, with the tacit assumption that this is a scheme of things that we mortals
find we cannot settle for. Eliot never says, "We can't settle for
this." We know that, as well as he does. So we follow him
from the opening lines on into a sort of spell—"Footfalls
echo . . ."—and thence into a vision where *memory* seems to
be operative, summoning things that one would have thought
were gone forever (Eden, and the whole fabric of beauty and
tranquillity that memory tries to salvage). Then the *thrush*
(not Eliot, as it were) tells us, "Go!", because to loiter in mere
vision, or memory, would be to be enchanted, like Keats'
knight-at-arms, lost to reality. The vision itself "points",
and the thing to do with anything that points—an arrow or
someone's forefinger—is to follow it. And we find this jumble,
cheek by jowl with that blissful garden. How so?

Because this is the way life presents itself to us. *But*—in this
section II of "Burnt Norton" we come upon a whole sequence of *cases in point* (not symbols) of *pattern*. Oh (we are
watching the sculptor). So, despite what seems to be mere
jumble out here in the nuts-and-bolts world of actuality (as
opposed to in that tranquil vision, say, with its box circle and
formal pattern), we find that pattern is omnipresent. We may
note here also that Eliot has not abandoned the problem of
time, changing topics and heading off in all directions, from
the garden to this chariot in the mud. It may seem a bit early
to tip Eliot's hand, but at that risk, let us say that *Four Quartets*
testifies to the notion that the Way ("up" or "down"—remember his Greek prescript) to Reality is to be found *via*
time and all that belongs to it, namely, our history, our mortal
life, and our daily experience. Those last couple of lines of
mine should probably be in boldface capitals, since they stand

starkly over against all forms of *escape*. Gnosticism, Oriental religions, Platonism, and our own reveries invite us to fly from the prison of time and the flesh to some eternal and "spiritual" (read "disembodied") state of affairs untouched by change and decay. But Eliot, being a Christian and a sacramentalist, believes that the physical is the very mode under which we make our way along to our destiny (*telos*) and that the effort to shuffle off the physical, or to deplore it, is both misbegotten and disastrous. (For readers unfamiliar with the term, a sacramentalist is one who believes that the points at which eternity touches time are physical points: Creation; Noah's ark; Moses' tabernacle; the Incarnation, entailing as it does a uterine wall, a gestation, a parturition, a circumcision, water turned to wine, a scourge, thorns, splinters, nails, a corpse, a body up from its tomb, a taking of that body into the eternal Trinity, and a Church made up of us mortals. This outlook is characteristic of Roman Catholicism, Anglicanism, and Orthodoxy: Protestantism tends toward the disembodied, focusing rather on the great abstractions of divine sovereignty, grace, atonement, justification, and worship that shun as much as possible the physical and that focus on the cerebral. Hence the centrality of the sermon in Protestant worship.)

That is too long a parenthesis, but it needed to be said somewhere. Back to the garlic. Just when we complain that the wheels of our chariot are driving heavily, we are hailed with "The trilling wire in the blood", forsooth. Attentive readers will discover in the next few lines, however, that there is a sequence of things (cases in point) that exhibit pattern. The circulation of the blood, for one. It keeps flowing despite "inveterate scars", that is, of wounded places that would seem to have covered the hurt up with mere scar tissue. But a scar is no "redemption": it just patches the thing up. Redemption must mean the virtual "re-doing" of the thing, so that the wound (any wound I have ever had, physical, emotional, circumstantial) is no longer there at all. The wars in which I was wounded may have long since been forgotten: but the blood, vibrating and quick, like electricity trilling through a telephone line, is alive and warm and, at least for the moment, "appeases" those wars. We will find, a few lines down, the word "reconciled". Reconciliation is a true restoration, whereas appeasement is a mere stopgap.

Eliot quietly uses the word "dance" to refer to this formal movement of our blood, round and round our bodies. It is not a word he lit upon in any offhand way. The Dance is the ancient notion, very common in the Middle Ages and the Renaissance, that Everything-there-is participates obediently in a universal choreography, beautifully designed and executed. Stars, clams, the west wind, atoms, the seraphim, you, time, raspberries, dolphins, and golden retrievers all have steps appointed to them, which they alone can execute. The perfection of the clam is not that of the west wind. The excellence of a star is not interchangeable with the excellence embodied and manifest in you. The dogs, glorious as they are, cannot do what dolphins can do. The word "Dance" gathers the whole created universe into one harmonious and solemn perfection, the word "solemn" used here in its old sense of the joyously festal that is ultimately serious—at the opposite end of the spectrum, so to speak, from the frivolous, the fatuous, or the inconsequential. (Readers may find this whole topic spelled out in C. S. Lewis' *The Discarded Image* [Cambridge, 1970] and on pages 17 and 21 of his *A Preface to Paradise Lost* [Oxford, 1970].)

This lymph here. Very Eliotean. He loved a quality in seventeenth-century metaphysical poetry of which Dr. Johnson complained that "the most heterogeneous ideas are yoked by violence together". This juxtaposition of garlic and sap-phires, or lymph and stars, jolts us. Exactly. We need jolting. We like to hum along as smoothly as possible; but of course to Eliot, as to any serious poet, part of the job of poetry is to *wake us UP!* Come. Lymph? Not in a poem, *please*. Let us save that for the X-ray room.

No (says the poet): let us have it here. Why? Because it is a case in point of what I am talking about, namely, pattern. It is no use talking only of the heavens (stars) if by that we wish to escape from what all gnostics and transcendentalists deplore as "the prison of the flesh". Eliot believed in *la carne gloriosa e santa*—the holy and glorious flesh, not the profane and re-grettable flesh. The lymph system is as perfect a case in point of pattern as is "the drift of stars". One thing echoes another.

And if we will "Ascend to summer in the tree" (summer is when all the leaves are there), we will have a vantage point from which to see not only the lovely pattern of shadow and sunlight in "the checkered shade" (Milton), but also—steady now—the pattern of *the boar hunt*.

Eliot keeps pushing his pen across his paper. Clot, scars, lymph, stars, leaves, boar hunts—we feel outraged perhaps. This is Eliot's conscious tactic: not frivolous outrage, such as we might find in black comedy, but rather the jolt that is needed, again, to wake us up to what is merely true.

We don't have boar hunts any more; or, at least, we don't have kings with all their splendid meinie coursing along the sodden floor of Polish forests in the great solemnity of the boar hunt. But in that great dash and confusion, hounds baying, horses snorting, capes flying, and the boar grunting and wheezing—even there, there is (or so thought those kings) a pattern. The horses do this, and the hounds do this, and the boar does this. We may be on the side of the boar (I myself am); but an undeniable choreography presides over this hunt, just as it does in our lymph system. Eliot is not the slightest bit concerned here with animal rights, or ecology, or fastidiousness (although he was himself a most exquisitely fastidious man). His poetry commands all. Time; vision; jumble; pattern: we must scrutinize all of it if we are going to get where we are going in *Four Quartets*.

Well, right now we are heading toward the point where all of the foregoing is "Reconciled among the stars". Hum. How so?

Is it not that while we are peering narrowly at anything, it may be difficult or impossible to get "the big picture", whereas if we back off, we can perhaps descry the pattern. There may be a vantage point among the stars from which, looking back at the world, which has so confounded us, we might gain this perspective. (It is too soon to say so, but we have already tipped Eliot's hand a bit, and it may bring some solace to readers vexed with these difficult lines, and more especially vexed with the suspicion that Eliot is going to paper over what any rational man can clearly see is plain chaos, to say two things here. First, the *Quartets* come to a close with the notion that "all shall be well"; and second, no one need fear that we get there by sweeping gritty reality under the rug. Nothing is swept under any rug in Eliot. Either things mean something, or they do not. Either there is a choreography, or we have a mere mess. Eliot is on the side of the former hope. Once more, a long but necessary parenthesis.)

Emerging from the brief lyric that opens section II of "Burnt Norton", we come upon a sentence fragment. Eliot does this. Being a poet, he can take liberties. And we find that not only is nothing lost by this violation of basic syntax: starkness is gained.

"At the still point of the turning world." We have all been told by the mathematicians and physicists that there is an unmoving point at the exact center of any wheel, or axle, that is not moving. The whole thing moves *around* that point. So. The world, in the sense of this globe upon which we find ourselves, *and* the world in the sense of the totality of human experience, has at its center that point around which it turns. The point is still. It is "neither flesh nor fleshless": that is, we are not excluding either the physical world (which most of us suppose, in our lesser moments, to be the "real" world) or the nonphysical, that is, the world of spirit, or of theory, or of fancy. And "from" and "toward" won't help us, since they belong to the world of *measurement*, or geography. No. It is the still point around which the entire dance (Eliot does not capitalize it *yet*) moves. In a highly compressed sense, it *is* the dance, since from it emanate all the movements there are. It is not itself movement: but "arrest" or "fixity" won't do, since these words imply—well, just that: arrest or fixity. But this is a vibrant point, the wellspring of all movement. And it is here that past and future are gathered. Is it "up there" somewhere? Not really, since the picture of "ascent" is too limited and plays into the hands of the transcendentalists, who wish for the loftiness of the escape *up*. Likewise with "decline": certainly the notion of the depths is a powerful one, intimating the profundity of human experience. But that, too, will not quite do for Eliot. The thing is, "there is only the dance", and without this still point, there would be no dance. The dance is Everything-there-is; and Everything-there-is is not haphazard. Obviously *Four Quartets* is already inching toward a certain answer to the question "What is it all about?"

We return to the fleeting glimpse caught in the vision in the garden. I can't locate it, but "location" itself, hemmed in as it is by either geography or time (past, present, and future), falls short.

The nine lines beginning with "The inner freedom" describe the state of the soul often alluded to by saints, most notably Saint John of the Cross. One has been freed from "practical desire"—the state, embarrassingly familiar to all of us, marked by "I wish" or "if only" or "I must have", and so forth. One has been released from both the scurry of action and the torment of suffering—suffering understood in the sense of *passio*—the undergoing of something. Eliot was, of course, wholly familiar with the ancient discussion as to which is better: activity or passivity. Martha or Mary. At the still point, those distinctions have vanished. What are here are both the energy and intelligence of the whole choreography and the vibrant stillness at the center. No "compulsion" harries us here.

Eliot now has to find ways of hinting at what *is* here, as well as what is *not* here. In this state we are "surrounded / By the grace of sense, a white light still and moving". Grace has come to rescue us from mere vacuity, which might follow upon this emptying of compulsion and desire. What is the "white light"? Surely it is that pure luminosity that suffuses everything in the precincts of *holiness*. Again, it is too soon to introduce this word: but out here in the world of mere prose (which is what my lines are, as opposed to Eliot's lines), one is obliged to state things rather flatly and to give away some secrets. Right now, Eliot summons the notion of white light for his picture. Later on, this same state of the soul will turn up as darkness (Saint John of the Cross is full of "the dark night of the soul", which is not the darkness of hell but, rather, the necessary removal of clarity and the acid test of faith, asking faith to forge ahead unable to descry the towers of the City of God anywhere in the distance). *Erhebung*. Again, Eliot's lofty assumption that we all should know our German. The word suggests an elevation, or a lifting up, an exaltation. But it is "without motion", since we are at the still point.

"Concentration / Without elimination." This might serve as a superscript for the whole of the *Quartets*. The poem is marked by an almost insupportable density (concentration), without eliminating anything—as would be the case, say, with a lesser poet who, hoping to carry us aloft into some tranquil region, excludes from his poem everything harsh, clashing, noisome, noxious, or discordant. We are certainly in "a new world" here: but lo—the old world so familiar to us, with all of its jumble, is here made explicit. Things begin to be *reconciled*. The ecstasy that marks our greatest pleasures while we are in this mortal coil is only "partial". And the greatest horrors are also only "partial".

An attentive reader might at this point shout, "Auschwitz! Partial? It won't do!" Well, supernally difficult to grasp as it may be, if what Eliot is inching toward is, in fact, the case, then yes—Auschwitz itself will turn out to be *not the end of the story*. If all time is unredeemable, then of course it is, and there is no "partial" about it. But we are being pushed on toward the realm where "all shall be well". But it is no cloud cuckooland, scoured of all agony and filth by fantasy. It is the state of affairs at the still point. So far, it is incomprehensible and unimaginable. Everything in us clamors for justice, which cannot come into play for the dead of Auschwitz unless time is redeemable. Does Eliot suppose that time, somehow, will be run backward and all injustices and horrors "remade"? He does not use that vocabulary. We may phrase our question that way, but for the moment we have to follow the "deception of the thrush".

The four lines beginning "Yet the enchainment" might themselves serve to crown the whole of the *Quartets*. This "past and future" that enchains us (we are obliged to submit to the inexorable march of *time*) and that is "woven" into the very frailty of our mortal flesh, which weakens, decays, and dies, turns out—get this—to *protect* us from both heaven and damnation.

What? I can't see how my being mortal and limited can protect me from damnation; and I don't *want* it to protect me from heaven, God knows. Well, yes, Eliot would say. The point is, we cannot "endure" these titanic ultimacies, heaven and hell. We are ready for neither yet, and we may give fervent thanks for the limitations that belong to our flesh, since if Reality (either heaven or damnation) were suddenly to loom upon us, we would be destroyed altogether. Our true and proper way lies *via* time and the flesh, not by a flight *from* them, as the Gnostics and transcendentalists and Platonists would have it.

The thing is (next paragraph), this parceling out to us of past and future, bit by bit, defends us from too much "consciousness". We have to take it as it comes. We could not sustain the sudden epiphany of Reality. We can only sustain "a little consciousness", thank heaven. We would have to be outside of time in order to get the whole picture, and we can't get out there (yet). The best we can hope for are these fugitive hints, which adumbrate Reality. Eliot once more conjures some haunting pictures of the fleeting state of consciousness that stands on the cusp between mere time and Reality. The moment in the garden: "The moment in the arbor where the rain beat, / The moment in the draughty church at smokefall"—these flecks of vision last only in our faculty of memory.

What arbor? The arbor that shows up in that line, that's all. And what's this "smokefall"? There is no such word. No: but Eliot, the poet ("makers" is what Aristotle called poets), can make up the word, and none of us need be in any confusion as to what it means. High noon? No. Rosy dawn? No. The quivering heat of mid-afternoon? No. It is twilight, probably the most apt time for this sort of haunting vision. We are harried by such intermittent glimpses of what seems to hint at immortal tranquillity: and the glimpses are useful. But we may not loiter in the precincts of mere vision, much less of hallucination, which is what all drug-takers seek and which, as we know to our sorrow, destroys us eventually, blissful though hallucination may be at the moment.

"*Only through time time is conquered*" (italics mine). It is yet another line that could be used as a superscript for the entire work. Time is the dimension appointed to us mortals. We are not angels. Everything in us rages against time, with its cold power to carry off everything we treasure—beauty, youth, peace, bliss. If only we could shake it off. The transcendentalists try to: but Eliot, the Christian sacramentalist, will have none of that. Somehow, strangely and even infuriatingly, time, cruel as it may seem, must be the very agent of our salvation. (It may be noted once more here that Eliot never raises his voice. There is no rage, no fury, in his poetic voice, and certainly no lachrymose self-pity. All is lapidary, we might say—inscribed inexorably in the stone of truth. Eliot said more than once that poetry, far from stoking emotion, provides an *escape from* emotion. Ha. That's not what *I* think. Well, it is what Eliot thinks.)

III

This section is one of the grimmest in all of the *Quartets*. We find ourselves willy-nilly in this time-ridden world that is our appointed place. It is "a place of disaffection". We are restless here, in this murk ("dim light"), with this remorseless

sequence of "time before and time after". It is not the clear
light that illumines things in the quick shafts of vision, "In-
vesting form with a lucid stillness", that is, bestowing the
clarity and repose on the "forms" that constitute our world,
touching even "shadow" with at least a temporary beauty—
say, the "shadow" of some disappointment or heartbreak perceived as itself a hint of that final state of affairs when those
shadows will be revealed as organic components of Beauty. If
we could handle and turn over ("rotate") these things, the
way a jeweler handles a diamond or a greengrocer a perfect
Bartlett pear, we might suppose, only briefly, that the object
suggests permanence. But no. Nor is it the "darkness to purify the soul" (Saint John of the Cross again), in which the
very "deprivation" of sensual pleasure serves a higher joy and
in which we are cleansed from the quixotic affections that
rush about seizing upon merely temporal objects—say, fame
or wealth or a great romance. (Incidentally, readers may observe in every line of my script here the genius of poetry:
Eliot distills all of this busy verbiage into short, purified lines.)
This frustrating sequence of before and after is too flimsy
to support either fullness ("plenitude") or vacancy, both of
which qualities must be brought to bear on the state of affairs
that teases and eludes us so long as we are trapped in mere
sequence. Plenitude: here is that hilarious dragooning of
everything into the service of beauty so much celebrated in the
baroque and the rococo. Vacancy: that Carthusian stillness
which itself, paradoxically, testifies to the same perfection
bespoken by the image of plenitude. It is always that way with
the Eternal: no single word or strategy will quite capture it.

What we find in this temporal mortality under which our
existence must move toward its end is "Only a flicker". What
is it that one sees in the ten thousand faces in the commuter
train, the supermarket, the doctors' waiting rooms, or on the

beach? They are "strained" and "time-ridden". What furrows the brows and creases these faces with crows' feet and dewlaps? Time. Disaffection. They are, alas, *"Distracted from distraction by distraction"* (again, my italics). This is surely one of the bleakest lines ever written. What a ghastly perdition this is. Here or there; hurly-burly; higgledy-piggledy; hodge-podge; chasing the swamp fires of a thousand distractions lest the stillness settle over one, and one is obliged to consider the "overwhelming question" (which Eliot's J. Alfred Prufrock wanted to avoid at all costs). Let us pack our minds with fancies, never mind how utterly meaningless those fancies are. Anything but Reality.

A terrible series of pictures follows here. "*Tumid* apathy." The very apathy of these distracted souls is diseased and swollen. They have given up trying to concentrate. And then "Men and bits of paper, whirled by the cold wind / That blows before and after time". Modern painting testifies to this. Mankind, supposedly crowned with the majesty of immortality and godlikeness, is reduced to being whirled like the trash that blows about in Times Square on a dismal Sunday morning after the bacchanale of Saturday night. And, as long as we are speaking of wind (says Eliot), it is all too much like the fetid halitosis that inhales and exhales from "unwholesome lungs", the very rhythm of the breathing beating out mere "Time before and time after". "Eructation": this rotten breath virtually vomits itself out.

If we were reading prose, we could insert the word "crowd" after "torpid". They are in a stupor, so debauched and degraded are they by their exhausting pursuit of distraction. Like those bits of paper, this crowd is "driven on the wind that sweeps the gloomy hills of London". The following place names are stops on the London Underground, and they are *not* Bond Street, Green Park, and Oxford Circus, where one might at least find some *attractive* distractions. These were, for the most part in Eliot's day (Hampstead has its charms), pretty grim neighborhoods. Once again, we need not ask Eliot how he got us here. The imperious drive of his poetry simply summons the Underground with its load of weary humanity as a case in point of the tumid apathy we are already talking about.

Then (my italics again)—"Not here / Not here the darkness, in *this twittering world*". Twittering. No, no. Not that. Twittering is, at best, for Paul Klee's birds. Surely we men are something more than that? Well, it doesn't seem so, says Eliot. We have come to the nadir, it would appear. This calliope of distraction is *not* "the darkness" of Saint John of the Cross, in which I might—I just might—encounter Reality.

If we are going to shake ourselves free from the fatuity and torpor that distract us from pursuing our true End, we are going to have to "Descend lower", to a depth far deeper than the tunnels of the London Underground. It will be "the world of perpetual solitude", which alone is the place where we can begin to face the ultimate questions. Eliot describes this region as a "World not world", and, as though to drive home the point, he follows this with a repeat: "but that which is not world". It is the deepness we must traverse if we are ever to leave all the twittering distractions behind. The words we encounter in the next lines are very Eliotean, but, at the same time, they bespeak the state of the soul so familiar to the saints: "deprivation . . . destitution . . . Desiccation" (dryness); "Evacuation . . . Inoperancy". All desire, fancy, sensuality, and property must be abandoned for this daunting pilgrimage toward the truth about our destiny. "This is the one way"—presumably the way *down*; "and the other / Is the same, not in movement / But abstention from movement;" The way *up* has the same destiny as the way down and, paradoxically, requires the same stillness. We must recall here that we are in a region of the soul to which neither preposition, "from" nor "toward", will help, since those words have to do with a measurable distance or length, whereas here we must be still.

". . . while the world moves / In appetency, on its metalled ways / Of time past and time future." Appetency: this is the only time in a lifetime the reader will come upon this word. It means what it seems to mean, namely, the state of being driven by desires or longings for this and that. Certainly the outer world, where men and bits of paper are whirled about by the various winds of desire and distraction, is ruled by appetency. But the soul must descend and leave all of that behind. The "metalled" ways are paved roads: in England, a metalled road is an asphalt road. Hence the suggestion here of busy traffic. The grass cart-tracks of the country, with their pastoral overtones, would not serve Eliot here. The rush of "time past and time future", which whisks everyone along, occurs on the metalled roads of life. We have got to step aside from that rush.

IV

In each of the *Quartets*, the fourth movement occurs as a brief lyric. And in each case, it echoes, sometimes from afar, it would seem, something of what has been at stake in the foregoing lines. Perhaps the key word in the little lyric we come upon here is "buried". There is no getting around that word: death arrives in the poem.

The foregoing descent—and deprivation, destitution, des-iccation, evacuation, and inoperancy—belongs to a state of affairs where business and preoccupation and distraction have long disappeared. Eliot's quiet tone is, really, quite brutal, if, that is, we wish to fend off the stark truth and opt instead for distraction. But that will not help in the least, as it turns out. "Time and the bell" are going to bury the day in any case. The bell is the bell in a clock tower, or in the church tower ringing for evensong: it doesn't matter which. And of course it may be said that with the coming of twilight, any given day is buried. Gone. Gone into the dark.

Or again, a similar dark chill can be achieved by a cloud's obscuring the sun. Suddenly our lovely picnic finds itself shrouded. The heralds of darkness threaten our pleasant diversion, so easy to carry on as long as the sun is shining on us. But now we must pack up. The fun is over.

What about this sunflower? We all know that sunflowers do, in fact, follow the sun with their faces, from dawn to dark. Insofar as it turns to *us*, it is saying, "Yes: you, too, come under the same passing from sunshine to darkness that we flowers must obey." There is a bitter irony here, in that *flowers*, so innocent and cheerful, become, without the smallest alteration in their behavior, the harbingers of darkness (read "death").

And what about this clematis? Again, a lovely climbing vine, full of pretty flowers. Ordinarily it climbs *up*, of course—up gates and doorposts and trellises. So pretty. But apparently nothing, not even pretty flowers, offers itself as an escape from this implacable darkness that is overtaking us. The trouble is, in these alarming precincts, the clematis itself might just possibly bend *down*—toward *us*. Oh, dear: everything is colluding here to drag us into the darkness. The very word "clutch" is frightening. If I find that this delicate vine seems to be clutching at me, I am profoundly disconcerted. Flowers are pretty, and harmless, and speak only of happiness. I don't like the way these tendrils seem to be clutching at me.

Yew trees are very commonly planted in old English churchyards among the graves. It can almost be maintained that if you find a yew tree anywhere at all in English poetry, the poet has death up his sleeve. And where are we, that these chill fingers curl down on us? We are in our coffins, six feet down, among the roots of the yews. The wood of the coffin has rotted away, and our skulls are exposed to these fingers. The quiet and fastidious Eliot never once blinks. He neither raises the hue and cry nor papers things over in order to spare us. *Four Quartets* merely testifies to how things are. We find it frightening only insofar as we are determined to remain in the state of distraction.

But then there's this kingfisher all of a sudden, in the same line. The kingfisher was the bird of "halcyon" days—idyllic days—in Greek mythology; and, if you know the bird, you know his habit of streaking, chattering loudly, just over the surface of babbling mountain brooks. His wings catch the glints of light coming through the forest trees—"answering" light to light: the light on his feathers answering the light of the sun. And then he is gone, and his chatter with him. Silence. Nevertheless (Eliot makes no sentence break here), "the light is still / At the still point of the turning world". The turning world of the sunflowers and clematis and king- fishers—*and*, it may be remarked, of all the distractions that distract us—turns only insofar as there is a still point at the center of all movement, and it is that still point to which we must come if we are not to be forever whirled and whirled. The turning world is not *bad*: that is, it is indeed the world crisscrossed by metalled roads of appetency: but it is also the lovely world of sunflowers, clematis, and kingfishers. But, says Eliot, there is *no escape*, even among the lovely things, from our End. The choice is ours: either to opt for perpetual distraction and hence blunder on to that End and find it to be calamity or to "descend" toward the still point and find *light*, not eternal darkness. Eliot's word "still" here presents another rich ambiguity: the light is still (always) there at the still point; and the light is very still (unmoving) at that central point.

V

The fifth movement of this *Quartet* gathers up all that has gone before it in the first four movements and introduces some new material. It is very much like what one finds in Mozart, Beethoven, or Bruckner. We have here movement versus stillness; life versus death; stillness versus sound; the beginning versus the end; and, the new material—words.

After all, Eliot's material is words, as marble is the sculptor's and notes the composer's. It is not as though words are *mere* instruments or just the lowly handmaidens of *meaning*. Words *are* the thing. When we visit Chartres, we do not dismiss the stone and glass as the mere stuff of something infinitely greater than stone and glass. The cathedral *is* stone and glass. It does not exist at all without stone and glass. We cannot drive any wedge of *meaning* between the materials and the glory to which the building testifies. The whole thing *is* glory, under the particular species of stone and glass. The same goes for notes in a concerto or divertimento, or swipes of oil and pigment in a Vermeer. The material constitutes the modality under which we perceive the thing itself.

"Words move . . . only in time." Well, obviously. By the time you get to the end of your sentence, the first word has moved into the past—into another time. It is the same way with music. You can't whistle the briefest melody without carrying on the enterprise under the scepter of time. Your first note is gone by the time you get to the end of even the first bar. So—we are still coping with time here in Eliot's poem.

There follows, in the same line, after a mere semicolon, a strangely sybilline remark: "but that which is only living / Can only die." Is this not painfully obvious? But depend upon it, Eliot is not given to larding his poetry with superfluous platitudes. Perhaps we could put the matter this way: Eliot's poetry, like alchemy, takes the lead of platitude and transubstantiates it into the gold of significance. Or, to change the metaphor, in Eliot's poetry, we are drawn up into the exceedingly rarefied sphere of the crystalline heavens, so to speak, where things we had never particularly noticed, because they were so utterly and embarrassingly commonplace, suddenly appear in all of their sparkling solidity. Good poetry, we have to keep in mind, most excruciatingly with Eliot, does, in fact, distill words as we ordinarily throw them about in daily chit-chat and raise their very substance to inexorable significance. "Transubstantiate", "distill", "raise": the very difficulty of addressing the matter in my prose here illustrates the point. Eliot's poetry does all of that simply by taking words (as Mozart did notes, or Vermeer pigment) and making something significant (and beautiful). Prose has to prowl about the outskirts, like a guide with his bunch of tourists. The thing itself stands there.

So: "that which is only living / Can only die." A flat commonplace. The irony is that we caper along never landing in the main clause—"Can only die." Distracted from distraction by distraction, we blithely leave out the adverb "only". There is one destination for that which is only living, and that destination is death. Time is the agent of the implacable movement toward that End.

But words, even after they have passed through Eliot's lips (or from the nib of his pen), "reach into the silence".

Somehow the statement stays there. Somehow it conquers time. The words are not obliterated. They are, to be sure, in the *past* (we're back to the first line of the whole poem), but they possess a strange and stubborn quality of imperviousness to the leeching of time. Oh. We're getting somewhere in this poem. The very fabric of the thing (words) calls into question the sovereignty, not to say tyranny, of time. They have a way of remaining, of not merely being buried.

But, "Only by the form, the pattern, / Can words or music reach / The stillness, . . ." Pattern, eh? Our lymph system and the boar hunt. Things arranged so that both meaning and beauty emerge. Like gardens. Or the Dance.

This Chinese jar here: there is an exceedingly intricate pattern of vines, or dragon's tails, swirling all over it. It could be said that it displays a "busy" pattern: but of course nothing is moving. The perpetual "movement" of the pattern moves only in stillness. A case in point of vitality, so to speak, which exists in perfect stillness and which remains, whatever is going on about past, present, and future. It may have been made three thousand years ago, but here it is. Do not call it fixity, since the pattern is vibrant. But, like the still point of the turning world, it is a vibrancy that, in a paradox, is synonymous with stillness.

It is not quite the same as the stillness of the violin, when the violinist has lifted his bow up from the strings and the note still vibrates briefly, although there is a similarity, since Eliot says, "Not that only. . .". The thing I am speaking of (he says) is a co-existence: the busy swirl on the jar co-existing with the utter stillness of the jar. The violin note is *something* like that, in that it does pierce the present/past/future barrier, if only for two seconds.

The next three lines, beginning with "Or say. . .", are as lucid as words can be. The "end", that is, the finished jar, or the whole sonata, *or the end/meaning/destiny of anything that exists in time*, is there before the potter starts potting, or the composer starts his pen. The whole thing, end and beginning, was always there, even before work started, and after the thing is finished. Plato would like this. The *idea* of the jar, or of the sonata, is "there", in some timeless state; but it appears under the species of time insofar as we mortals may encounter it. Smashing the jar, or leaving the symphony hall, does not annihilate the thing in the ultimate sense. Both the jar and the sonata were, are, and always will be "there"—perhaps in some absolute sense, but certainly in our memory, which (back to section I) is the faculty in us that summons and inhabits the past and obliges it to present itself in the present.

"And all is always now." This is beginning to sound suspiciously Buddhist or Taoist or perhaps Hindu. And certainly Eliot had done his homework in Oriental religion. But as a Christian sacramentalist, he does not have the luxury of denying the pat reality of this world of jars, etc., nor of the real, as opposed to illusionary, passage of time. It is not absorption into the Whole that he bespeaks, nor mere appeasement of this sad draining away of the things of this world. There is a "point" where things are "reconciled". Our nostalgia for the past and our wish to find some way of conquering mutability are true cues, not foxfires. So far, we are a long way from the end (End) of the *Four Quartets*: but Eliot is nudging us along toward a fruition in which everything—*everything*—is gathered up and appears in all of its splendor in the Dance. Nothing will be swept under the rug; and there will be no lachrymose regretting of the "dear dead days beyond recall", nor any mere absorption or obliteration of the adamantine actuality of each thing into some universal and diaphanous Whole.

My prose needs a paragraph break here. But Eliot's poem

admits of no such thing. In the same line with "all is always now" we find (following a period, to be sure) "Words strain . . ." Here is the poet's *agon* (wrestling). Words are the very materials that Eliot is employing to mount a "raid" (this word will show up later) on this riddle of past, present, and future, with all of the loss that that sequence seems to assume. It is a riddle insofar as it is *there* and undeniable: but then the deepest reaches of our being shout "No!" to it and will not leave it alone. The task Eliot is requiring of his words is so hefty that the poor things "strain, / Crack and sometimes break, under the burden, / Under the tension, slip, slide, perish, / Decay with imprecision, will not stay in place / Will not stay still". How are we to keep from laughing with sheer delight at this glorious marshalling of verbs? I don't think Eliot would take offense. After all, words are his marble, pigment, sound waves, or choreography, and to see anything under any of these modes accomplished with such utter verve, bravura, and perfection does, in fact, call out from us the selfless laughter of pure joy.

But of course it is agony. Words, splendid as they are, especially in Eliot's hands, *won't quite do it*. Neither will Michelangelo's marble, Vermeer's pigment, Mozart's sound waves, or Balanchine's choreography. There is always some cacophony trying to wreck the enterprise: our wandering thoughts, or the melancholy habit of words to slip into mere cliché, or our stupid flattening out of the eminence of sheer meaning—whatever. "Shrieking . . . Scolding, mocking, or . . . chattering": these are the enemies of poetry, as dripping water is the enemy of marble or someone muttering in the audience is of Mozart's flute sonata. Alas! the poet seems to say: my materials are not quite up to the task.

Perhaps not *quite*, we readers might murmur, but very close to it. *We* aren't complaining, dear Eliot. Carry on.

And here, with no preface, much less apology, we come up against "The Word in the desert". Hey, nonny! The Temptation of Christ? Come. This is too long a leap. We cannot possibly follow you, dear sir.

Yes. We can. That is, if we have paid the smallest heed to how Eliot pursues his craft. He summons cases in point from the four corners of the universe, insofar as they are, in fact, cases in point. And the assault on Eliot's poetry by chaos, or the breakdown of meaning, or our own meager resources, is analogous to the assault that was made on The Word Incarnate by that avatar of chaos, Satan. His tactics are tedious, pettifogging, and inconsequential in the presence of the titanic Articulateness that stands there. And, as it was with The Word, so it is with the word of poetry. The "temptation" always seeks to diminish and ruin the sheer force of *meaning*, which words serve. All shrieking and chattering and so forth.

I have never been happy with my own effort to make much out of this "shadow in the funeral dance". It could be that what we want is silence, or at least solemnity, in the "dance" that presides over all exequies, and this "crying" is disorderly. This seems severe, since who will forbid us to cry at the funeral? But of course my crying is a more or less uncontrolled surge of emotion, whereas the rite that presides over the funeral itself is a stately and well-ordered business. It may indeed be punctuated by sobs, but they are just that: punctuation that is not in the score. Or this crying shadow may be a phantom flitting in and out of the Danse Macabre, spoiling its solemnity. (The Danse Macabre, or Dance of Death, is an old, especially medieval, picture of our mortal life, in which we all appear in a line, holding hands, and led by Death toward the grave, the idea being that whatever diversions—distractions, if we will—may mark our *lives*, it is all something of a mummery in that it all collapses into the grave anyway.)

In other words, this crying shadow is one more case in point of a spoiling interruption. Likewise with the "disconsolate chimera" with his loud lament. The chimera was an odd beast who scoured on and off stage in ancient and medieval tales, always apparently looking for something and never able to find it. Naturally he is loudly lamenting, and naturally that interrupts Eliot's words, or any words that are trying to say something orderly, or The Word in the desert.

"The detail of the pattern is movement . . ." We have seen this in the Chinese jar—the details do, in their motionless way, bespeak movement. "As in the figure of the ten stairs". Once again, we want a footnote, and Eliot gives us none. So we mull the thing over, trying to keep our musings closely in tune with the poem. Of course *any* stairs "move" in the sense that they "go" from downstairs to upstairs. They have no purpose at all other than movement. But they themselves are motionless. Again, a case in point of motionless movement. We might cite here Saint John Climacus ("of the ladder") or Saint Bonaventure or other ancient writers on the spiritual life who describe the soul's advance toward beatitude under the figure of steps, or stairs, or mansions. In every case, it is the same: we *get* somewhere by means of something that itself does not move. Back to the Still Point (perhaps it is time to start capitalizing that Point). The wheel gets us from here to there; but at its dead center is the unmoving point.

"Desire itself is movement / Not in itself desirable. . . ." This is strong stuff here. We have all accused somebody of being in love with love. The rhapsodic young swain sighing over a strand from his leman's golden locks. Or the silly thirteen-year-old, girl or boy, who is desperate to be in love, no beloved one having showed up at all. The desire is both powerful and sweet: but, says Eliot, it is not in itself desirable. Certainly the same would be true of sexual desire, else why would people buy pornography? The very arousal is a plea-sure—but not actually desirable, if we will put our minds to it. Eliot wishes to distinguish here between desire, so univer-sal and so domineering, and Love, which, like the Still Point, "is itself unmoving". It is only "the cause and end of move-ment, / Timeless, and undesiring. . . ."

And once more we find Eliot nudging us very quietly along toward a further idea. The Love toward which the *Quartets* move is the thing that lies at the far end of all lesser "loves" (desires). Passion, romantic love, infatuation, fraternal or paternal or maternal or filial love, patriotism, attachment to an old family house: these are all loves. Love itself is the object of all desire, but it is not itself desire.

"Except in the aspect of time / Caught in the form of limitation / Between un-being and being". Here is yet again the crux with which Eliot is coping in his poem. We mortals only apprehend The Thing itself in a fugitive, intermittent, spasmodic way—"Quick now, here, now, always— . . ." (see below). Vision may hint at It; a love may hint at It; the dragon's tails on a Chinese jar may hint at It; the funeral dance may hint at It. But that is all we can get—"Hints and guesses" (again, more on this presently). Why? Because we are "Caught in the form of limitation / Between un-being and being". Caught in the limitation of time, in other words. Or put it this way: time is the *form* (the shape; the frame) in the very limited dimensions of which we catch the fleeting hint of eternity. We are perched, so to speak, on the cusp between un-being and being. Between that "time" when we *weren't*, and the state of affairs when we will have fully arrived at "being", that is, at the fullness of being for which we mortals are destined.

"Sudden in a shaft of sunlight. . . ." In the next five lines Eliot augments the picture. The thing—our fugitive, partial, intermittent grasp of the eternal—may occur, say, in a moment as fleeting as a shaft of sunlight slanting through the window, illuminating the little dancing dust particles (what my infant son once called "sunshine crumbs"). The sight of this may trigger the hidden children's laughter, which we heard in the garden, which laughter was itself a tag end of Eden, so to speak. Be alert ("quick") to apprehend it. It's "here, now, always—". That is, if you stay alive to the whole enormous business addressed in *Four Quartets*—the teasing mystery of being mortal while all the while you are made for eternal Joy—there won't be a moment or an event or a place where you won't find your sleeve plucked by this mystery. And, in the light of this, how dismal, even ridiculous, is my lot if I merely shuffle along through time, blind, deaf, and shrouded by ennui, which is precisely what most of us do (back to the Greek superscript: "Although Reason [our capacity to draw inferences from what we encounter] is common to all of us, most of us live as though we had a wisdom of our own"). Time, in that case, is just a long, sad vista, "Stretching before and after". I have missed the present, which is the only "point" at which I have the chance to glimpse Reality.

East Coker

I

The title of this section is a tiny bit more auspicious than was the title "Burnt Norton". That is, when the house burns down, there is, in effect, nothing left. But in the parish churchyard at East Coker, to which Eliot traced his forebears, and in which his ashes rest, we do have something, even if it is the ashes left behind by a man. Actually, Eliot's ashes rest in the wall of the church, or at least that is where the plaque is. But the church-yard is full of coffins containing whole skeletons: not much more auspicious than the ashes of a house or a man, but nonetheless stark reminders of that which *has been* and which, one might venture to hope, *still is*, and still has a destiny—a *future*.

That may well be reading much too much into the title. We may settle rather, if we wish, for the simple fact that the village of East Coker is still alive and has a history reaching back in time. The past, then, is made present somehow by East Coker. The village—any village—is a meeting point of past and present. And future, of course, since it has some sort of "tomorrow". Eliot himself, when you come to think of it, existed in the "future" of the East Coker in which his ancestors lived and worked. Or we might drag this out one more step by observing that Eliot is now in the "past" (he is dead) of the present village. Once more we find that poetry severely distills prose's efforts to say the thing.

The opening, brief sentence of this section is a variation

on a quote attributed to Mary, Queen of Scots, as she mounted the scaffold to be beheaded at the command of her Protestant cousin, Elizabeth I. Mary is said to have remarked, "In my end is my beginning", thus testifying to her Christian hope that this "end"—the scaffold—marks the beginning of the real, indestructible, eternal destiny for which she was created. If you turn her words around backward, as Eliot has done here, you get the same thing. In my beginning (my birth) my end (my destiny) is already embodied. The full oak tree is the end closeted in the acorn. This strikes the note for "East Coker", like a tuning fork.

We find, now, the obvious, although, as is the case with all great poetry, it is "what oft was thought, but ne'er so well express'd". You don't get new information in poetry, the way you do in a physics class. You simply find, in perfect form, what you already know. In this case it is the commonplace fact that houses are built and eventually crumble, or are enlarged, or removed so that the highway department can bulldoze a cloverleaf (a by-pass). The reader scarcely needs any help with the next few lines. It sketches out the immemorial cycle of nature. It may be remarked here that "house" is also the term used for dynasties, as in the House of Habsburg or the House of Windsor. These, too, disappear eventually. Time past and time present. . . .

This opening paragraph ends with five lines that echo the famous lyric in Ecclesiasticus about a time for this and a time for that. They also exhibit Eliot's habit of giving us the unexpected and vivid picture. Fancy conjuring for us the wainscot (sort of a chest-high baseboard panel) behind which the field-mouse *trots*! There's poetry for you. In a phrase we are whisked right in to the ancient, vacant house. Or castle, as it might be, where the tattered *arras* (tapestry) moves in the wind blowing through the vacancy. What's this *motto*? It might be *Ne me impune lacessit*, or *Honi soit qui mal y pense*—hoary mottoes embroidered into the tapestry designating old families (the Montresors, from Poe's *The Cask of Amontillado*) or ancient honors (the Order of the Garter). For the hundredth time, past and present conflated.

So. In my beginning is my end. With no transition at all (which is how life presents itself to us, we will recall), we find ourselves presently in a lane. Anyone who has traveled in England will know these tiny lanes, barely wide enough to let one car squeak through. On each side are steep, ancient embankments, surmounted by equally ancient hedgerows, thus making the lane "deep". It seems to be a late afternoon in summer, with the light "falling" across an open field (you can glimpse these fields intermittently where a gate is cut into the hedge), the heat "electric", the light "sultry", with a warm haze brooding over it all. Very soporific. Even hypnotic. If a van (panel truck, for Americans) passes, you have to lean back against the bank to let it pass.

The lane "insists". How so? Well, it "points", shall we say—thus summoning an Eliotean word we have already learned to note. We have no option in this lane—no choice of various directions. The lane insists that we must move along toward the village. The very stones (we may glimpse a Cotswold manor house through one of the gates) seem to *absorb* the light, not rebuff ("refract") it. The whole confluence of heat, light, stones, silence, and haze seems to wrap us in a seamless fabric that may very well have us dropping off into a dream, what with the sleeping dahlias and the owl just waiting until the twilight deepens.

Now. In that open field—but don't come too close: you might frighten the little figures away—we are about to witness a most enchanting vision. Eliot, with no apology or transition, lands us presently in the seventeenth century, at a nocturnal village dance, with music supplied by "the weak pipe and the little drum". Men and women, the local farmers and their wives, are dancing around a bonfire: obviously some established and solemn local custom. The lines that describe this dance Eliot has lifted whole cloth from the writings of Launcelot Andrewes, bishop of Ely and Winchester and court preacher to James I. Hence the archaic spellings.

This dance signifies matrimony. Not that it is a wedding feast, by the way: *any* traditional dance (we may set aside entirely the jerking movements that have, since the 1960s, preempted this old and noble word, "dance")—any traditional dance signifies matrimony insofar as it exhibits the exquisite, patterned, joyful give-and-take that marks true marriage. The lovely steps of traditional dance, either folk or ballroom, constitute a playing out of the motions of love itself—now I advance and you retreat; now I step back and you advance—all of it *solemn*, in the Middle English meaning of that word, indicating that which is at once both joyous and freighted with significance. It connotes the opposite of frivolity, mere spontaneity (which is good in its place and so far as it goes), and disorder. So here are these seventeenth-century country farmers and their wives enacting in their midsummer folk dance the same harmony and solemn joy that we find in the "dignified and commodiois [sic] sacrament" of marriage. Given this picture, the reader may follow the next few lines without further commentary.

What about these "loam feet" though? Well, for one thing, our feet *are* made of loam, as it were, and will return to loam after our death. But besides this, the loam is simply the earth that clings to the farmers' clodhoppers. This country mirth, with no punctuation at all, is drawn right down under the earth, nourishing the corn. To put it baldly, their decomposing bodies enrich the earth from which new life (corn, in this case) arises. Once again, Eliot is not delicate. It's the "flesh, fur and faeces, / Bone of man and beast" that we ran into in the opening lines of "East Coker". Of course, the farmers and their wives are "Keeping time" in the dance—you have to, or else the dance turns into a pushing, struggling ganglion of people. But they are also "keeping time" with death (the Danse Macabre), as they did in "their living in the living seasons". Life and death: the rhythmic cycle. Eliot echoes again the sequence from Ecclesiasticus about times: the stars' movements, milking, harvest, copulation, eating, drinking. "Dung and death". This is not the bitter conclusion of some disenchanted cynic—"Well, that's where it all ends anyway, so what's the point?" We find out in the next line—a fresh paragraph.

"Dawn points." *That's* the "point". Whether it is a verb or noun, the word fits Eliot's task here. We always have "the still point" in our minds as we read, but we are beginning to find that things—everything?—*point* to something. The lane "insists" that we go this way. Now dawn points. To another day of heat and silence. And (no paragraph), "Out at sea . . ." How did we suddenly get here? By the same transportation operative all the way through the *Quartets*: the poem moves, and we move, as past, present, and future do. We find our-selves presently in a whole new situation, perhaps with no very discernible connection with where we have been just now, but here we are. While the cornfields are awakening to another day of summer heat, and the lane insists on pointing us to the village, out at sea "the dawn wind / Wrinkles and slides". If you have ever stood on the shore or at the rail of a great liner, you already know that this is precisely what the wind does with the surface of the water. It wrinkles the water into millions of tiny wavelets, and the gusts whisk (slide) across the water, ruffling and speeding the wavelets in little hurrying patches. So. "I am here / Or there, or elsewhere." Right. The thing is, the same oddity lands us here or there or elsewhere in ordinary life, but the "overwhelming question" that Prufrock was so afraid of is always staring at us, wherever and whenever we are. And it's all "In my beginning". Who of us will boast that he has reached the end, or even approached it, if by "end" we mean the fullness of being that is my ultimate destiny? No. It is safe to say that I am in my beginning whether I am an infant or a nonagenarian.

II

The next seventeen lines, in octosyllabic iambic meter, with only a sketchy rhyme scheme, are, to my mind, perhaps the strangest and most difficult lines in the whole poem. I can only venture what efforts I have made, with much scratching of my head.

What *is* the late November doing with the disturbance of the spring? The words themselves (we haven't got any punctuation yet, so it's not a sentence) bother us severely. Well, it (November) has defied the ordinary sequence of *time* (past, present, and future) and decided to turn warm, in an Indian summer. We are supposed to look for flowers and the animals that have been hibernating ("creatures of the summer heat"), in the *spring*, not in November. Something has wrenched time out of its ordinary track.

Remember that Eliot is inexorably obliging us to move along in his poem, while the poem itself endeavors to cope with the progress of time. But, as happens, neither life nor time is always trustworthy. We are nettled to find, say, Indian summer, when we had already got out all our boots and ski jackets. Nothing seems trustworthy. What *can* we trust? An excellent question, and one that lands us squarely in *Four Quartets*, where the whole paradox-ridden business of life is addressed and—we hope—given poetic shape.

So let us receive this late November as we should (if we are on the road to sainthood) receive any interruption. Let us receive it and see what we get.

We get snowdrops, for one thing, "writhing" under our feet. The cold weather of November has made sorry work of these flowers that try feebly to hoist their colors at the beck of Indian summer. And of course the word "writhing" we don't like very much. It conjures pictures that we would like to huddle offstage. Eliot is always ruining things this way: an innocent country dance, and before you know where you are, it's dung and death. And now pretty flowers, writhing, alas. The time is out of joint. The hollyhocks have gotten "leggy", as the horticulturalists say. Too tall. And their brave scarlet trumpets are getting grey and falling down, in spite of Indian summer's efforts to simulate springtime. Here are some roses—filled with *snow*. A sudden flurry has interrupted the interruption visited upon us by the Indian summer.

Then we get some high and mighty lines. The "Grand March" from *Aida*, we might say (which is not at all the note ordinarily struck by Eliot's quiet and implacable verse). Thunder, stars, triumphal cars (Assyrian chariots, shall we say, rolling in victory into Nineveh), and all of this grandeur "deployed", as it were, not in insignificant earthly skirmishes with Babylon, but in great cosmic conflict. There's some Brobdingnagian cataclysm afoot. Scorpio (the zodiac sign) is fighting the Sun, and so forth. Once again, the reader may stagger through the following lines in the light of what we have glimpsed so far. (Leonids, by the way, are meteors.) Fancy comets *weeping*. Something must be dreadfully out of

order. And it's all whirled in a vortex (like the Maelstrom—
the great whirlpool) that will suck us all down through the
apocalyptic fire that will melt the universe before the ice takes
over. Ice, of course, hints at absolute zero, which is what you
get when all movement has ceased. The Norsemen, as well as
Dante, saw ice as the *final* ruin.

What, then, are we to make of this wild lyric stuck, it
would seem, here in the middle of Eliot's otherwise apparently moderate and prosaic lines? Well, perhaps it's a bombshell. Not Eliot's usual tactic, but with this lyric he boosts us
in to an intimate look at the desperate difficulty facing the
poet as he tries to make words match the frightening reality
he is addressing. For, let us face it, the whole of this four-part
work *is* frightening—like Dante's work. It is all about death,
and the overwhelming chances of our missing our cues by
distraction, and about the beatitude that *is* in the cards if
we will gird up our loins and attend to the "hints and guesses"
that adumbrate that beatitude, and also about the dark interstellar spaces into which we may tumble through mere
inattention.

As it turns out, Eliot or, shall we say, the poet working on
this poem: the two are not necessarily synonymous; after all,
Eliot wrote those lines, and left them in the poem!—but let
us just say that Eliot does not like that bombshell approach.
Bombast is not his style. So, we'll have another go at it. "That
was a way of putting it—not very satisfactory. . ." Has any
one of us ever read a poem with that sort of line in it? The
poet turning to us from his desk, as it were, and saying that?
Hardly. The thing this poet doesn't like is "periphrasis"—the
roundabout way of saying things. Nor does he like hackneyed
poetical fashions, which, far from startling us awake, only lull
us (tra-la, tra-la, tra-la), leaving the poet with the whole job
to do over again if he wants his poetry to have any force to it.

It may surprise us to hear about this "intolerable wrestle / With words and meanings". At least it will surprise us if we had supposed that poetry emerges if we just scribble down any windy lines that flit through our imagination (which, alas, seems to be the idea behind all undergraduate attempts at verse).

And how can a poet as serious as Eliot expect us to believe that "the poetry does not matter"? We will come upon more about this in "Little Gidding", where the poet, speaking with the "familiar compound ghost" (Dante?), learns that indeed the poetry does *not* matter, in the light of the Reality that the mere poetry bespeaks. But the poets have to keep on trying; otherwise language will sink into mere Dadaism, and all discourse will have collapsed, and the ice will have taken over.

Eliot has omitted the period at the end of that half line about the poetry not mattering. Surely this is a typo, or a lapse in the poet's attention? Hardly. My own guess is that what we have there is the poet brushing aside the statement as a mere remark, spoken sotto voce, if we will, and tailing off while he starts over, and barely asking the dignity we accord a punctuated sentence.

What was not what one had expected? The thunderous culmination of everything he had tried to evoke in that bombastic lyric. A great, crashing apocalypse that would suit the immensity of all the questions raised about the passage of time: houses crumbling; dancers turning to mold; the destiny of all the strained, time-ridden faces; the fugitive nature of the moment in the draughty church at smokefall; and so forth. Surely all those questions call for comets weeping and Leonids flying? I mean, it's all so *gigantic*.

No. Or no, if we expect such rodomontade to confirm for us the immensity of the stakes. Well, then, "What was to be the value" of the time, long anticipated, when old age with its wisdom might speak to us and lay to rest the terrible questions? (Readers will once more be reminded here of how mere prose lumbers next to the agility of true verse: read Eliot's lines again. The prose does not matter.) Are we to understand that all the mollifying nostrums the elders may have offered us about "autumnal serenity" and life culminating in great tranquillity were just whistling in the dark? *Deceit*? All that serenity: Will it turn out to be only hebetude (a lovely Eliotean word, meaning dullness or lethargy)? Are the wise old men, who should have gained wisdom, only ladling out for us "secrets" (ha), which are useless when it comes to penetrating "the darkness into which they peered / Or from which they turned their eyes"? Chances are they rather swiftly averted their eyes after making one nervous attempt to peer into the darkness. Who can abide the *nada*?

The thing (which *Four Quartets* is talking about) is too abysmal for dodderers to cope with. All the savvy that these old men may have picked up from experience has (a crushing understatement, very Eliotean) "only a limited value". The trouble is, that level of "knowledge" forces a piddling pattern of its own onto That Which will not yield to the effort. But we've got to get this Unconditioned that looms upon us— we've got to get it *manageable*, for heaven's sake. We can't live with these cumulonimbus clouds of Ultimacy hanging over us. . . .

We might have to. And anyway, if you clamp your little pattern onto it all, you will miss entirely the operative thing about *the* pattern, namely, that it parcels itself out to us, so that we mortals can cope, every moment. We can only take these bits because even this parceling out is terrifying, being, as it is, "a new and shocking / Valuation of all we have been".

Oh, dear. Good, kind Mr. Eliot, spare us. Your poem is turning out to be as insupportable as the Last Judgment, and we don't need that.

But the poet goes on speaking, quietly, implacably. All of this "wisdom" of old age is actually the somewhat inconsequential business of our unlearning the deceptions that gilded our youth with false hopes. Foxfires. They didn't do too much harm, as it happens: but our merely unlearning them will scarcely answer in the face of this abyss into which we prefer not to gaze.

The next four and a half lines are not a sentence. We should be getting accustomed to this habit of Eliot's by this time. The unfinished sentence has an unnerving way of simply landing something in our laps, quite unapologetically. A main verb makes the thing manageable (or so we wish). The tactic belongs to the serene and peremptory tone that Eliot needs. We can't tuck the matter into the "whole-sentence" pigeonhole. It dangles, the way Reality dangles, eluding the grammatical net—or any other net.

Where are we, then? "In the middle." Readers will recall the first line of the *Divina Commedia*—"In the middle of the road of life . . ." It's actually all the way, for Eliot, not just in the middle. Here's a dark wood (Dante again); a bramble (hard to slash your way through); a *grimpen*, forsooth. This is a bog, which Eliot picked up from Conan Doyle's *The Hound of the Baskervilles*. One wants to avoid it at all costs. The trouble with it is that you can't get a foothold (much as the old men would like to plant their feet firmly in some cliché). And not only that: you are menaced by monsters—a huge hound, in Conan Doyle's tale, but any monster from Dante's hell, too. "Fancy lights" flit and glimmer: will-o-the-wisps. Deceptions. A will-o-the-wisp always leads you farther into the bog, never out of it. You will doubtless end up positively enchanted here, again like Keats' wretched wight. Hell is murky, says Lady Macbeth again.

So "do not let me hear / Of the wisdom of old men. . . ." It is fatuity. Escapism. Fright. Flat platitudes, all in the interest of fending off the Inexorable. The thing is, these old men are *afraid of fear*. Of course they are. Bridge. Let's have a game of bridge. A drink. Pour me a double Scotch. Bonhomie. Ha ha ha. Anything to wave away these "sad and stealing messengers" (Hopkins). Besides, we don't want to be "possessed", by senile dementia, or by nightmares, or by terror. And heaven deliver us from "belonging to another" (the jailer, or the nurse, or the warden) or to "others" (the orderlies in the nursing home), *or to God*. The final terror—the apotheosis, ironically, of all of our efforts to dodge him, since of course he calls everything into question, most notably our silly tactics of avoiding him.

It looks as though the only genuine wisdom, then, has got to be humility. Be it done unto me according to thy word. Behold the handmaid of the Lord. This is the only wisdom, and it will not fade, nor let us down.

Double space in the poem. Space in which we may collect ourselves and pull ourselves together to face the bald truth. The houses are all gone under the sea. The dancers are all gone under the hill. What did we expect? That things would frolic along, somehow contriving to avoid dissolution? If that is what we are telling ourselves, then Eliot is wasting his time, and it may be that God is wasting *his* time.

III

Here comes a very alarming section of the poem, although it ends on a note not so much alarming as quietly insistent.

Readers should have no difficulty with the first nine lines. When men die, they go out into the dark. That would seem patent. The jolting thing about Eliot's particular listing of death's conscripts is the (typically Eliotean) "unpoetic" nature of the roster. All these successful citizens. The Almanach de Gotha is the register of European royalty and nobility. The Directory of Directors (there is one) seems particularly ironic.

And of course we all go with them. But what about this "silent funeral, / Nobody's funeral, for there is no one to bury"? Well, for a start, most funerals *are* silent, more or less. Not much clashing and clanging of cymbals and so forth. But "*Nobody's* funeral"? You have to have a body for a funeral, surely? Yes, but the point is that by the time you tot up all the funerals there are, you find yourself concluding that *whose* funeral any particular funeral is is unimportant. They are all the same. Dead men are, as far as this world is concerned, Nobody. "No one to bury"? Again, this duke or director or distinguished civil servant has joined the anonymous ranks of the dead. We are burying a nonentity.

So, says the speaker in the poem, "I said to my soul, be still, and let the dark come upon you. . . ." That is, since the darkness is *going* to envelop me anyway, suppose I *will* it to come? That changes everything. We come, here, to something like Saint John of the Cross' "Dark night of the soul" or the *Nada* sought by various Eastern religions. But Eliot is speaking, of course, from a Christian point of view, so we may stick with Saint John. In his work we find that the path to the knowledge of God is going to require the total emptying of myself—the busy querulous self that chatters away, distracting me from distraction by distraction, and that would rather have the sand of the inconsequential thrown in its eyes than ever to clear them and peer into the Dark. If I will invite the darkness, it will turn out to be "the darkness of God".

The "Dark, dark, dark" of the first line is transfigured from being the fathomless black abyss of vacuity to being the ascetical Way to the Beatific Vision. Either of these two "darks" is wholly calamitous to my distracted self: but the one is perdition, and the other is salvation.

We now find three extended images, or, to remain faithful to a point made in the opening pages of this study, three "cases in point" of the dark—indeed, of apparent nothingness.

First, we have the scene in a theatre, when, at the end of the first act, say, all the stage lights go out, and the house lights are not turned on. So we sit there in total blackness. But we can hear the sets rumbling on and off up there on the stage as the stagehands change the scenery. If we squint, we can just manage to descry a blackness up there that is slightly blacker than the auditorium—"a movement of darkness on darkness". That is the sets being moved. And we hear "a hollow rumble of wings". The sets rumble off into the wings. But of course Eliot knows perfectly well that nobody can read about such wings without thinking of the wings of the Angel of Death. You are entirely correct, Eliot might say to us. It is not either/or. Take your pick. Both sets of wings come to the same thing, for both waft away all the familiar scenes that we have hitherto known—during Act I, or during our lifetime. That splendid backdrop with its hills and trees and great façade that we applauded when the curtain went up is gone. All the places I have loved over the years, from childhood on up, are gone.

Or perhaps we might think of the sepulchral silence that descends on the passengers when the subway (it is the Underground, or the tube, in London) makes a mysterious halt between stations and the lights go out. Come. How long are we going to sit here? What's wrong? I'm running out of things to think about. The stillness and blackness are beginning to oppress me, I must say. In fact, "Help, ho!" If Saint John of the Cross were sitting here in this marooned carriage, no doubt he would be perfectly serene. But I—I find distraction to be infinitely more insistent.

Or again—that strange time when I was anesthetized for some surgery. There was a period, either when I was sinking into oblivion or when I was struggling out of it, when I was *conscious*, as it were, but I couldn't frame any concrete thoughts. I seemed to be suspended in a sort of vacuity.

Eliot puts the following lines into the mouth of "I", but it might at the same time be Saint John of the Cross whose voice we are overhearing. It is a very strange sequence of admonitions we hear, though, since it appears to reject hope, love, and faith—the three theological virtues of the Church—virtues that, we might have supposed, would carry us through this undoing of everything.

So might run the plausible objection. But we are into a region here that leaves mere plausibility behind. The thing to do here, apparently, is to disencumber myself from *hope*, for a start, since what I would most certainly conjure by way of hope would be "hope for the wrong thing". Just get me out of this, please, somebody. No. Not that way lies your true hope. Well, surely I cannot be asked to divest myself of *love*? That is the queen of virtues. Fair enough; but your whole imagination is clogged with the love of this, that, and the other thing. That must all be expunged if you are going to move toward the love of the right thing. Well, faith, then . . .

All right. But "the faith and love and the hope are all in the waiting". Bustle is out of the question here. Let whatever faith, love, and hope you have disengage themselves from all the trivia to which they have been attached, and concentrate them solely on this waiting. In fact, you have to wait without *thought*, too, since if there is one arena busier than the rest, it is the arena of thought. What are required here are stillness and nothingness. You, my soul, are not yet even "ready for thought", since the thoughts fitting to the blissful precincts that lie at the end (*telos*) of your being are, so far, unattainable.

If you will follow this rigorous program, then, and only then, will you find that this "darkness shall be the light, and the stillness the dancing". It all sounds oddly familiar, and rightly so: we encountered it in the Greek superscript at the beginning: "The way up and the way down are the same." Many paradoxes. But what do we suppose the region of ultimate felicity is like, since it outstrips all of our mightiest suppositions? Paradox seems to be perhaps the only way to approach it at this point.

"Light" and "the dancing" hint at that felicity, certainly. Radiance suffusing and gilding that solemn choreography which lies at the infinite pole from hell's entropy.

Or shall we invoke the garden again? The wild thyme, which we can only scent. Readers will recognize the enchanted region of *A Midsummer Night's Dream* here. The laughter of the children in the shrubbery. Oh—if one could only find the gate into that world. The mere echoes of that ecstasy may break my heart. . . .

No. It is not all lost. But neither is it handily regained, that "first world". There are requirements: death and birth. Both entail agony, as we all know too well. But to die is gain. Except ye be converted and become as little children, ye cannot enter the kingdom of God. This, of course, is to skip too far ahead too soon. We have not heard tell of God yet. That would blunt the *point* of Eliot's poem.

We find ourselves running out of patience at this point, however. "You've said that already, dear Mr. Eliot", we mutter. Fine. I shall say it again. Perhaps you have not altogether grasped it all. "In order to arrive there . . ." Oh.

But wait: this is nonsense: "To arrive where you *are?*" I'm already where I am. Come.

Ah, but this "are" is not just your contingent existence here, in time, at this juncture of your biography. This "are" is ARE. That unimaginably blissful state of fullness of being that is your End. So far, you may be said to be "where you are not", that is, where your poor existence is a mere NOT next to that glorious ARE.

The journey there is going to deprive you of ecstasy, just in case you were thinking that it's all just a yellow brick road. Dante had to go down to the bottom in his itinerary. The next nine lines ring the changes on this theme. Readers will scarcely need much assistance here. We find six antinomies listed: know/ignorance; possess/dispossession; *what* you are not/through the way *in which* you are not; do not know/the only thing you know; own/do not own; where you are/ where you are not.

Once again, the swift economy of poetry mocks the laborious trudge of prose.

IV

And now the fourth movement in "East Coker", the lyric. Readers will notice that Eliot, uncharacteristically for him, brings rhyme and iambic meter into play here. Ordinarily he shies away from this sort of thing because the danger there is that we will be lulled. But the words are so lacerating in this lyric (like a surgeon's scalpel) that Eliot no doubt judged that we need some balm in the form of rhyme and meter.

How did we get into this operating room? The same way

we get anywhere in Eliot. We simply follow him, into a garden, after a boar hunt, into the Underground. Right. But this wounded surgeon bothers us. We would prefer a man in full control of every nerve and muscle in his body, not someone maimed.

But of course there is no such thing as an *un*wounded surgeon. Every man has suffered cuts and scrapes and perhaps even broken bones in his boyhood, and certainly every man has been wounded by life itself: disappointments, heartbreak, fear, anguish of one sort or another. Ah: so the surgeon is not entirely indifferent to my plight under the knife here. He himself has been cut. So he plies his steel scalpel delicately, yes, but also implacably. He will not stop short of the deepest point to which it is necessary to dig in order to get at the trouble. Sentimentality will not hamper his work. His knife "questions" the distempered (diseased) part, asking, "Is it here? Here? There?" This is the attitude on the part of this healer, then—both compassionate and "sharp", that is, not afraid to cut to the root. But his *hands* are bleeding—yes. They have bled in their own day, certainly; and here it is *my* blood that covers his hands (or, in this latter day, the latex gloves on his hands).

We cannot, of course, hear about bleeding hands without recalling the Passion of our Lord. Bleeding hands, like the Labyrinth or the Lotos Eaters, belong to a given story, willy-nilly. But what is Christ doing here? Our question answers itself before we have time to pause: the hands that wrought our eternal salvation, not just our recovery from a tumor, bled. That Healer's art cuts deep (we must be crucified), but not before itself has been deeply cut.

The prose in this commentary is unfair, of course, since it plunks the cards on the table flatly, whereas the poetry of the lyric does not show its hand in quite this businesslike fashion.

It is the office of poetry to show, not to tell. Bible texts in the skein of this poetry would be like cannonballs in gossamer. The web would be in tatters.

The surgery resolves "the enigma of the fever chart". The chart, of course, listed symptoms A, B, C, and D. What do they add up to? Well, until we can get in there with the knife, we won't quite know. The symptoms are enigmatic. The trouble might be dire, or it might be almost nothing.

But surely Eliot has gone too far with the next stanza? "Our only health is the disease"? We are talking nonsense here. No. The only hope for health comes insofar as we say, "I am sick." The health follows this sad admission. And there is more: if we want to recover, we have to obey the dying nurse, whose job it is, not to pander to every whim of ours ("Couldn't I just have some coffee?" "I'd like a cigarette."), but to remind us that we are sick and have to stay with the regimen. But the *dying* nurse? This is worse than the wounded surgeon, until we recollect that there is no such thing as a nurse—or an anybody—who *isn't* dying. She certainly is not immortal. Well, then, she's mortal: dying. Eliot keeps jogging us with his lines, so apparently matter-of-fact and routine. And things are going to get worse before we get well.

That's a bleak outlook, surely? Just what am I suffering from, pray tell, if this is the prognosis?

You are suffering from "our, and Adam's curse".

Eliot lays a trump on the table. Original sin. Much worse than cancer or cardiopulmonary infarction. It will kill us, eternally. That is, unless we obey the dying nurse. Who is she?

Once again, I think we have to venture a guess here. Who *is* the "she", the assistant to the Healer, who cares for us in our sickness? Eliot was an Anglican churchman. My own guess is that she is the Church, which is made up, of course, of dying people, popes and all. My hesitation to draw this interpretation arises from my awareness of Eliot's extreme reluctance to indulge in this sort of "symbolism". I put that in quotes, since both the nurse and the Church are real cases in point of assistants to the Healer.

One other remark here: in this simultaneous reticence and bald frankness, we catch a glimpse of Eliot's whole poetic technique. There is nothing of brimstone preaching about it: but it summons us, in its very *politesse*, to the brink. Eliot was always the courtly man in the Savile Row suit, at a polar extreme from the sweating, ropy-necked, pop-eyed stump preacher. Nevertheless, he does not shrink from pointing to the flames.

The whole earth, then, is the region in which we are to be healed. Readers will recall here the last line in section II of "Burnt Norton": "Only through time is time conquered." That is, time, which drags everything with it into oblivion, *is* conquered, not, as the Platonists and Gnostics wish, by an escape from time, but *in* time. Likewise, the *place* of our healing is *here*—in this life, on this earth. This is where the drama of our salvation was played out in real geography (Galilee and Judea), in real time (*sub Pontio Pilato*), by a real human being (the Incarnation). The whole earth is our hospital.

But who is this millionaire who has endowed it? There is a grim irony here, I think. The millionaire is Adam (he had everything), but alas, his endowment to us is the curse—sin, sorrow, suffering, and death. However, if we do well, "we shall / Die of the absolute paternal care / That will not leave us, but prevents us everywhere".

Readers may get lost there. Can we put it like this: "Die", by this time in the lyric, is our death to sin and death and hence our birth into Everlasting Life; and it is God who embraces us with his paternal care, never leaving us, but rather going before us all the way ("prevents" is an archaic usage, meaning "precedes").

Quite unobtrusively, Eliot's quiet voice has landed us on the dizzying heights of theology or, rather, of the Gospel. Any mere Freudian or Jungian or deconstructionist reading of these lines strays sadly from Eliot's manifest intention. The lines will not yield to the tactics of postmodern criticism.

When you are dying, which we are, "The chill ascends from feet to knees". Mistress Quickly noted this about poor Sir John Falstaff when she was attending him on his death-bed. The fever sings like electricity in our mind's "wires". And then again, suddenly, Eliot steps straight from the local and the familiar (after all, deathbeds are here, in our own town, and even in our own house, often) into the region to which all of this is the anteroom. The only lasting warming from this creeping freeze is purgatorial. One does not have to be Roman Catholic to stick with Eliot here. One way or another, either in Purgatory, as that has always been held by the Church, or via some purging process, I am going to have to be made ready for the Beatific Vision, the light of which may most certainly be supposed to "warm" us. Eliot's mix-ing of "frigid" and "fires" is traditional, and also Dantean. Whether fire or ice is the better picture, no one can finally decide. Either environment spells death to all that I fondly think of as "me". But "the flame is roses, and the smoke is briars". Put it backward: there are thorns in this purging to be sure, but that is merely the smoke from the fire—not the hottest element. The flames, which one is quite sure will reduce one to clinkers, being divine, turn out to be the very element of beatitude, whose bliss may only be dimly inti-mated by our bringing roses into the picture. (An analogy, not used by Eliot here, but familiar to all readers, would be the old picture of the crucible, which consumes all the dross and produces fine gold.)

To belabor the last quintain would be to discredit the reader. What we have is the Eucharist, which is our food, the only food of Eternal Life, even though in our lesser moments we find it pleasing to suppose "That we are sound, substantial flesh and blood". We are not. We need this salvific food. And, despite all of the gore ("dripping blood . . . bloody flesh"— Eliot is not reticent here), nevertheless we call this Friday *Good*.

V

In this section, Eliot returns to a theme he was pursuing in section II, namely, his struggle with the poetry itself. After the rising and falling of houses, and the peasant dance, ending in dung and death and the new dawn "pointing", and after the rather wild section about the late November, we will recall that, with no particular apology, Eliot sits back, as it were, and comments, with a certain apparent frustration, on the difficulty of getting the words to answer to the subject matter. This, of course, is always the core of the problem for the poet, perhaps in a way never quite experienced by even the best prose writers, for the simple reason that poetry demands above all an almost hydraulic compression of language that obtains quite differently when it comes to the work of the prose writer. In any event, we find it again here. Having spoken of "the intolerable wrestle / With words and meanings" in section II and, also in that section, having turned to the reader in reply to the reader's querulous complaint that he is repeating himself—not only accepting the complaint, but challenging it ("I shall say it again. / Shall I say it again?")—

Eliot forges ahead with the immensely difficult task of speaking about this "darkness" and the way down being the way up. And now again, after the extreme compression of the lyric about the wounded surgeon, the poet, perhaps without even looking up at us, forges ahead as though it is all of one fabric with his "topic", with a lament about how much time he has wasted between the two world wars, "Trying to learn to use words".

A superficial reading of the *Quartets* might lead one to suppose that Eliot is *interjecting* these asides about how hard it all is, writing this thing—punctuating, so to speak, his primary work with groans that might well have been expunged from the finished work.

But no. Clearly, in his mind, the poetry itself is of one fabric with the topic. Nay, it *is* the topic, which is why one was inclined to place quotes around the word a few lines back. Later on we will hear that "the poetry does not matter". What is this? Just a petulant flinging together of profound subject matter with these groans? Hardly. What we have, of course, is paradox, which, once again, seems to be the only tactic possible when finite language addresses the Ineffable. The poetry matters infinitely: I must get these lines exactly right; but then the poetry doesn't matter, since it, like everything else mortal, will decay and will all have to be done over again (we will come upon this melancholy business in section II of "Little Gidding"). Or put it this way: this *Way* ("up" or "down"—it is all the same) is really quite indistinguishable from the poet's labor with words. Is it taking our reflections too far here to recall that it was the Word that created all things in the beginning and was incarnate by the Holy Ghost of the Virgin Mary? For Eliot, the Christian sacramentalist, you can't drive a wedge between word and thing. The poet's labor with words is a case in point of the indivisibility of word and thing in the sacraments. He has to close the gap, opened by the banalities of our ordinary chitchat, between word and thing. We toss words about blithely, little caring whether there is any very neat "fit" between them and what we mean. (This has become a deadly pox on language in our own time, with the substitution of such phrases as "I go" or "I'm like" for "I said".)

"So here I am, in the middle way, having had twenty years . . . largely wasted. . . ." We sympathize with your complaint, dear poet, but isn't this a bit banal next to the dripping blood? Certainly a different pace is struck, the way Mozart may switch from *presto agitato* to *molto adagio*. But it is the same concerto. Before we enroll the word "banal", let us follow where the composer/poet leads us.

The first eighteen lines in section V, down to "The rest is not our business", are stark enough to obviate much commentary. But they also contain some of the most memorable lines in the entire work. The "raid on the inarticulate", for example. And "the general mess of imprecision of feeling, / Undisciplined squads of emotion", and "For us, there is only the trying", that is, the terrible difficulty of the poet with language, perennially making new starts, perennially failing, forever trying to get the better of words only to discover that, by the time he has got them, their referents have grown old, or else he himself is no longer disposed to say it that way. "Shabby equipment"—referring both to words, which doggedly insist on sinking into cliché, and the poet's own intellectual powers, which are very far from what he wishes they were. And the awful struggle to surmount the mess of imprecision: therein lies the Himalayan watershed between bad verse and good poetry—or between shoddiness in my inner man and the litheness that marks the interior figure of the saint.

(At the risk of obtruding here, I may say to the reader that trying to say something—anything—apposite about these lines has turned out to be for me a grim effort to get the better of words and, most assuredly, the discovery of my own shabby equipment. One feels that the whole attempt is a sad matter of trying to highlight a Van Eyck by spreading mayonnaise on it. Critics may justly suggest that I skip it then, to which I can only reply that I am following—very poorly—Eliot's own example of confessing his struggle.)

The further ironic difficulty about the poet's task is the bald fact that the mountain has already been scaled any number of times "by men whom one cannot hope / To emulate". What with Homer and Virgil and Dante and Shakespeare and Milton ahead of one, what is there left to do? One tries, "by strength", that is, by girding up one's loins and assailing the massif; and also "by submission", that is, by making one's words *obey* that which they attempt to address. It is a platitude, but perhaps worth repeating at this point, nevertheless: *the poet's job is never to hail us with new information.* That is the job of textbooks, newspapers, and lectures. Poetry always submits to what *is* and, at best, succeeds only insofar as it vivifies that which is and opens our eyes yet again to what is already "there".

"But there is no competition." Dante has done what he has done and has won the palm. Eliot's job is not to see if he can do it better and win the palm away from Dante. Both poets have the same job: "the fight to recover what has been lost / And found and lost again and again". Adam and Enoch and Abraham were as wise as Plato and Bonaventure and Kant, if we are speaking of *wisdom* and not just *information.* What is true remains so from one eon to the next, but we mortals keep losing track of it. The moral map of the universe can never be redrawn, whether by Euclid, Copernicus, or Einstein. The difficult part of the poet's task is to find a way of saying what Homer or Dante hailed us with, in an argot that is alive and not dead. But the further difficulty for Eliot is that he has to do it "now, under conditions / That seem unpropitious". The twentieth century, with its speed, its decibel level, its savagery, and its destruction of language as well as of civilization, scarcely seems propitious. Give me the slower pace of thirteenth-century Ravenna if you want me to write a poem.

But heigh ho: perhaps there is "neither gain nor loss". Perhaps one century presents obstacles as daunting as those presented by any other. Like the saint, the poet finds himself faced with the same syllabus that earlier saints and poets faced. For him, "there is only the trying. The rest is not our business." We can never quite get it said: it is God's business to crown the attempt with some measure of success.

But from whence shall we embark on this "new beginning", which, says Eliot, is the poet's perennial job? "Home is where one starts from." Where else? We all started there, and the older we get, the more baffling the world becomes. We have seen myriads of people, including our own family and friends, die. What sort of "pattern" can we descry in this dance "Of dead and living"?

For one thing, our cues seem to come, now that we are old, not so much from "the intense moment / Isolated, with no before and after", which we encountered in the garden in "Burnt Norton", but rather, now, from "a lifetime burning in every moment". There's a tall order for us. Sudden and fugitive glimpses of Eden are all very well, but they are not the prescription for the long haul of life. Such a glimpse might, if we are like Eliot, be vouchsafed to us. Most of us have to get on without these glimpses.

On the other hand, the prescription turns out, not so much to relieve us from the intensity of vision, but rather to demand that that very intensity mark "every moment" of our lives. But how are we to contrive to "burn" in every moment? We can't, of course, but then we are failing. There is no mention of the word here, but could it be that Eliot has introduced, very subtly, the notion of Grace in these lines? No one can burn in every moment. But my soul, having been ignited by Grace, may, in fact, be said to burn in every moment. Left to my own devices, I will always douse the flames. At the end of "The Dry Salvages", Eliot becomes explicit about this dilemma. "For most of us, there is only the unattended / Moment, the moment in and out of time. . . . These are only hints and guesses . . . and the rest / Is *prayer, observance, discipline, thought and action*" (italics mine). Hurrah for the moments: they do indeed furnish glimpses of what is Real. But the rest of our long march is drummed out for us by the hammer of those five activities. "Only through time time is conquered" ("Burnt Norton", II).

Eliot will have nothing to do with any nonsense about our floating off into a vacuous religious ether, nonsense that is always popular with fools, either in ersatz Eastern religion as that is tasted by Western dilettantes or in any of the voguish shortcuts to Nirvana that crop up every hour on the half hour in California. We are talking about a lifetime of immensely taxing fidelity here.

"And not the lifetime of one man only / But of old stones that cannot be deciphered". Whatever was going on at Stonehenge, or in the Temple at Karnak or Angkor Wat, or on the Aztec pyramids and Sumerian ziggurats, the whole lineage testifies to our unremitting effort to come at Whatever-It-Is. No "one man only", even Saint Francis himself, can exhaust the mystery, or fully reach the Beatific Vision, at least in one lifetime.

But what is this about the evening under starlight or lamplight? Well—those are "moments" vouchsafed to most of us.

In youth, we walk out, alone or with our beloved, to gaze at the stars. Very intense. In old age, we find ourselves sitting quietly by a lamp leafing through our photo album. Nostalgia may overwhelm us here. Fine. That itself testifies to time's passing, which is the one implacable fact that we cannot bring under any sort of control but which, says Eliot, is the victor over nostalgia's tears, since it is by this very passing, passing, passing, that "time is conquered". Even our senescence *can* be touched with flame. Now we have arrived at the "Long hoped for calm, the autumnal serenity" of "Burnt Norton", and let us hope most fervently that it won't simply go down the drain of "a deliberate hebetude". Uselessness. No. "There is a time" for this.

And anyway, "Love is most nearly itself / When here and now cease to matter."

Ah. Love. Very Eliotean, this: this way of very quietly placing bang in our path something immense. We have heard about love only in a few lines of warning in "East Coker", III: ". . . wait without love". Now we come upon it as though it were the thing toward which everything so far has been reaching. And that is correct. But Eliot is not the poet of trumpets and drums announcing big topics. He has already told us that ballyhoo is not to his taste: "That was a way of putting it—not very satisfactory. . . ."

Right. But what is this about love being most nearly itself when here and now cease to matter? Just that. The man in whom love has been perfected is at home in any place (here or there) and in any time (now or then). He has grown beyond the futility of nostalgia and wistfulness. He is as fully at peace under the lamplight as he was under the stars with his new beloved. No lamenting a lost youth for him. There is a time for this. It is appointed. The wise man of Ecclesiasticus has already told us so.

In fact, "Old men ought to be explorers." Even in the lamplight with a shawl around their shoulders, they "must be still and still moving / Into another intensity / For a further union, a deeper communion. . . ." "Here and there does not matter": the nursing home; the solitary cold-water flat in Putney; the royal bedchamber attended by wigged courtiers; the eremitic cell at the edge of a lough in Galway. None of that matters. The voyage is the same. The "further union, a deeper communion" is that state of affairs of which the prophets and saints speak, when we will be at one with the ecstasy bespoken in "Jesu, Joy of Man's Desiring", and in Dante, and in Teresa of Avila, and in John of the Cross, and the Lady Julian of Norwich, to whom Eliot turns at the end of "Little Gidding".

The way thither leads, of course, "Through the dark cold and the empty desolation" of old age. It leads us out from the Earth of "East Coker" to the next one of the Four Elements, namely, the Water of "The Dry Salvages", "The wave cry, the wind cry, the vast waters / Of the petrel and the porpoise". Alas. So I must leave all that is familiar and firm underfoot behind? But that will be the end of me!

"In my end is my beginning."

The Dry Salvages

I

It would be well to recall at this point that we cannot simply fix things so that each one of the Four Elements attaches strictly to one of the *Quartets*. Eliot is composing four *quartets*, which means that all four instruments (Air, Earth, Water, and Fire) play ensemble throughout. Naturally there are solo parts. But it is not as though Air has the score all to itself for the whole of "Burnt Norton", and so forth. As I have pointed out earlier, I am reluctant to insist on too rigorous an identifying of the four sections of the *Quartets* with the Four Elements, one apiece. That would be four solos. On the other hand, we cannot deny that one or another of these Elements seems to have the ascendancy in a given section. In "The Dry Salvages", certainly we are awash in water a good bit of the time.

From the title and Eliot's explanation thereof in the subscript, not to mention the wave cry, the petrel and the porpoise at the end of "East Coker", we might be forgiven for expecting to launch out onto the ocean here. But no. We find ourselves at a muddy river. Readers are free to suppose that this is the Don or the Yangtse or the Mississippi: it doesn't matter. All big rivers present the same challenge to the first men who try to cross them. It is also to be noted here that the river, like the country dance and the vision in the garden and the Almanach de Gotha and the shifting scenery in the

95

theatre, stands on the cusp, so to speak, between what *is* and what *was*. Time. Past, present, and future. The whole concern of the *Quartets.*

Eliot opens "The Dry Salvages" with the lapidary remark that he does not know much about gods. We perhaps are inclined to start a bit. Gods? Come. Who's talking about gods? And once again we find ourselves obliged simply to follow the poet. By this time we ought to have learned that he is likely to introduce anything in heaven, earth, or hell, without so much as a finger raised in warning or a rise in the decibel level of his voice.

So. Gods. That is how we are to think of this river. It unnerves us, since we who live in the epoch that has conquered rivers with mere engineering (bridges and tunnels and so forth) are disinclined to view them as a difficulty, much less as an insurmountable barrier. But the voice of this poet will not have it so. The huge river "Is a strong brown god— sullen, untamed and intractable. . . ." Oh, well, of course, if you want to think of it in those dire terms, I suppose you are free to do so, dear poet. But for myself, I find rivers quite unthreatening. One just spins across them on the Interstate in one's 300-horsepower SUV, and presto! One more state to add to one's travel list.

The trouble about rivers (as has been the trouble about surgical operations, and the London Underground stuck between stations, and lamplight in the evening quiet) is that they constitute hints and guesses, just as much as the intense and fugitive moments of vision. Hints about *what*? About what is perfectly plain, if we will simply wake up. Time is draining off into the past, the present will not stay still, and the future—what about that future? Is it to be the dark interstellar spaces? Certainly there will be a funeral—there is no getting around that.

So here is this river. It just keeps rollin' along, like Old Man River. Its silent and remorseless flow has something sullen about it. It won't speak to us. And certainly it is un- tamed: our bridges and tunnels have not made the smallest difference in the transfer of water from Montana and the Dakotas to New Orleans. And intractable. We can even put up an enormous dam if we want, but the water is going to keep on flowing *somewhere*. It won't quite submit to our schemes.

The first men to cross—Choctaws in canoes, say, or white pioneers with their Conestoga wagons on rafts—find the river patient to some degree: it will let them cross most of the time. But certainly it is a frontier. One is acutely conscious of *this* side and *the farther* side. It takes days to chop down the trees and tie the logs together into a raft. The river is also "useful" as time goes on: it bears the paddle-wheel steamers from the Ohio River down to the Gulf, with their loads of passengers or hogs.

But of course, with the progress of engineering, the river disappears, in effect. The problem is solved. City people even commute back and forth daily. Ten minutes, if the traffic keeps moving.

". . . ever, however, implacable". The river is not impressed with the spidery steel spun across it. It is going to flood in the spring whatever we do about it, destroying farmhouses, fields, cows, and even people who get in its way. Death: "what men choose to forget". In the rush hour, as I whisk across from my office in Illinois to my house in Missouri, my concern is getting on home for supper and Fox News. Death is not really my concern, thank you very much.

Insofar as that is true, then I am a fool. Perhaps I, one of millions of worshippers of the machine, am missing some- thing that seemed important to the primitive men who offered propitiatory sacrifices to the river. Perhaps they were closer to the frightening truth of the matter. This river, whether I choose to ponder the matter or not, is "waiting, watching and waiting". This poem of Eliot's is beginning to get under my skin.

And this "rhythm" of the river—spring flood, low water, ice in winter—this rhythm was also "present in the nursery bedroom". What? How? Well, time governs things in the nursery—birth and growth, for a start: the newborn infant is presently celebrating his third birthday. Night and day, for another thing. Breakfast and nursery tea. What are all of these but markers in the implacable march of time away from the past, toward the future and the funeral? Likewise with the April flowers around the front door, or the harvested grapes on the dinner table in autumn, or the family gathered round the gas lamp on the winter evening. Time *present* and time past . . .

So, "The river is within us. . . ." We, like it, are subject to the sovereignty of passing time. The circulation of the blood and lymph that we found in "Burnt Norton" obeys the same rhythm as does the river.

And now the sea. The thing about the sea is that, far more than the river, it is wholly ungovernable. It encircles the land (our safe habitat) on all sides, the way eternity encircles time, as it were. But it has a way of pushing *in* to the land, even where the shore is granite. We might have thought that the land's edge was a safe boundary. But the coasts of Maine and Norway, rock though they may be, find the sea intruding into inlets, coves, and fjords.

It seems a bit gratuitous for a commentator to say to the reader, "This next is a very beautiful section of poetry." But it is hard to refrain from such bathos with respect to the following lines about the beaches. Eliot would no doubt demur. I have worked on every word of my *Quartets*, and I do not consider it a service to have bits and pieces plucked up as especially "beautiful". He is right, of course. Nevertheless, there is no getting around the fact that, say, the second movements of Mozart's piano concerti nos. 20, 21, and 27 carry us away, or that the funeral dirge at the end of *Beowulf* is something that quite overwhelms us. But we need not argue the point.

The point about the beaches is that they spread out for us the record of thousands of years as we kick along through the sand. Not only ancient forms of life (I know nothing of marine biology, but I have heard it said that the horseshoe crab is a particularly ancient specimen), but also "our losses". The nets (a seine is a net), lobster pots, oars, and other gear are left here to bleach while the men who used them go into the dark interstellar spaces. Who can count the voices of the sea, let alone its gods? The whistle of the wind in the rigging, the soughing of the surf on the sand; the bellow of the waves around Cape Horn. And the many gods: Neptune, Proteus, the Kraken, Leviathan, Moby Dick, Scylla and Charybdis, the Maelstrom: very alarming it all is.

This immense entity, the sea, reaches inland to our very cottage doors: the salt on the briar roses, the fog, and the "howl" and "yelp" that one hears. All of this is exactly true on Cape Ann, Massachusetts, where I live within the sound of the sea and where Eliot's family spent their summers. You can even swear that you hear human voices at certain times. It is all both menacing and caressing: the same waves that whisper on the sand also grind on the rocks (the "granite teeth") of Cape Ann. There is a foghorn offshore here: whether it is the "heaving groaner" that Eliot heard a hundred years ago, I do not know. But it is there to warn the men who must round the headland as they point their yawls and sloops and lobster boats homeward. And over it all, the unremitting screech of the great black-backed gulls in their thousands.

The bell buoy clangs away with baleful iteration, measuring "time not our time". Our time is a mere matter of wristwatches and kitchen clocks and very high-tech chronometers. Morning, afternoon, evening; Monday, Tuesday, Wednesday. Small stuff. This bell *tolls*. You toll a bell for a death: the verb does not apply to wedding bells or fire alarms. The groundswells that were rolling across the face of the deep when the Spirit of God moved upon the face of the waters at the Creation are the agents of this tolling. You are all going to die, and we shall keep tolling, for those who have died thousands of years ago and for those who are to die in the eons when you have long since been forgotten. The bell clangs in obedience to these immemorial groundswells.

But we have skipped over these anxious worried women. They, of course, are the wives of the clipper ship captains whose voyages from Salem and Newburyport had them away from home for years at a time. Who of us is more agonizingly conscious of the terror of time than these women, awake in the small hours, calculating ("He should have been home a month ago"), trying to unravel the tangle of vicissitudes that bedevil any transoceanic square-rigger or clipper, piecing the past together with the future, which is, of course, a wholly futile enterprise, especially between midnight and dawn, when things take on a particularly gloomy aspect. The past seems a mere deception from this grim vantage point, since it has vanished; and the future may as well be "futureless", since "it may bring the news of my husband's drowning". The very cessation of time here before the morning watch, "when time stops", is itself never ending. "The morning will never come, much less the morning that will bring the ship and my captain home to me."

II

And now the second movement, raising the agonizing questions, as the previous two second movements have done. Where is the end of all this decay and wreckage? "There is no end." But before we get to the second stanza, we find ourselves halted. What, pray, is this "prayer of the bone on the beach"? Well, what is it? What *would* a bone pray? "O God, rescue me from this desiccated state of affairs. I am only a trace of the living creature that I *was*." That would be the obvious prayer of any and all bones, if they could, in fact, pray. But why "unprayable"? And what, *pray*, is this "calamitous annunciation"?

Eliot knows that he cannot bring in this word "annunciation", even with a lowercase letter, without everyone's recalling *The* Annunciation, which was certainly "calamitous" for the Blessed Virgin, since it upset every single one of her expectations as to how her life on this earth was to play itself out. And she responded with the (virtually) unprayable prayer: "*Fiat mihi*: Be it done unto me according to thy word", she says to Gabriel. For the rest of us mortals, our immediate response would be, "Oh, no! No. I'm not quite up to that. Go away." Her prayer would prove itself unprayable as far as we are concerned.

But Eliot's poem *is itself just such an annunciation*. With inexorable quiet, like the voice of Gabriel, it summons us to our End—both the end of all of our busy hopes about life and of all of our timorous defenses thrown up against the inexorable (we may recall here the poor sods "distracted from distraction by distraction") and, most notably, of our End, which is the *telos*, or fruition of our lives, which will, of course, oblige us to assent to its summons with "Oh. Well,

then (gasp), be it done unto me according to thy word."
There is no other way to the calamitous Beatific Vision. The
Way Up to Joy turns out to require the Way Down (abandon-
ing my pitiable array of distractions, assembled so anxiously,
like flimsy pickets, to ward off that Joy).

Insofar as I am merely wondering when all this wreckage
will stop, the answer is "There is no end". In fact, the passing of time only adds to the tally. My emotions sag into the
dismal business of pushing along, year after drab year, amid
the breakage of everything that I had fondly supposed to be
reliable. Since all of that "reliable" stuff—my preferences,
my friends, my money and family and career and health—is
the very stuff that time will obliterate, then, if I will sum-
mon up my courage, I will see that it is all of that which
is most fittingly to be renounced if I am to get on toward
my real End and not simply be left as another bone on the
beach.

And, of course, there is the final addition to this melancholy sequence of ruin, namely, old age. My pride sinks with
every bedpan and catheter the nurse brings in; I grow testy
over my failing eyesight, hearing, teeth, youth, and muscle
tone. I might try the tactic of refusing to "devote" myself to
anything, like the French existentialists, who faced their de-
mise quite coldly, but that is as stupid a ruse as all of the tactics
brought into play by more timorous spirits to frustrate the
inevitable. The boat is adrift, and leaking in the bargain. I
may take up Simone de Beauvoir's refusal to shout for help, or
I may join all the lesser spirits in shouting for help. Neither
option is of the slightest importance: we cannot stop our ears
to "the undeniable / Clamor of the bell of the last annunciation", that is, you are doomed.

Readers will need very little help with the next three
stanzas. They iterate our unremitting efforts to keep *going* in

the face of certain doom. The "setting and hauling" refers, of course, to the fishermen's wrestling with the sails. The word "lowers" is a verb pronounced to rhyme with "towers": it refers to the way storm clouds frown over us. The "banks" are ledges under the surface of the ocean, not the banks that hold the rivers in place.

The point is, we have to think of these fishermen as doing all of that, which at least has the *look* of something that has a point to it: we can't face the grim fact that, finally, one or another of their voyages will be "unpayable", in the sense that they will have no coinage with which to pay off the Angel of Death, and the "haul" from this last voyage, unlike the nets full of cod or bluefish, will have us averting our eyes, since what the nets have brought up now is Death.

There is no end of all of this: there is only, alas, this "hardly, barely prayable / Prayer of the one Annunciation".

What ho! A capital "A" all of a sudden? Yes. We all are the recipients of ceaseless annunciations, in the sense that not a single moment passes that does not bring with it some hint or guess of our End. But of course these lowercase annunciations that hail us oblige us to recall "the one Annunciation", where we hear the (to us) daunting prayer of the Virgin, "Be it done unto me according to thy word."

There is an overwhelming sense in which the next thirty-nine lines, which bring us to the end of section II, cannot be rephrased or even "explained", for the simple reason that what Eliot says here cannot be said in any way other than the way in which he says it. But the sheer compression of it all daunts many readers. They find themselves lagging behind, like inexperienced climbers trying to keep up with a nimble alpine guide. So, at the risk of finding ourselves plugging along in drifts of bathos, we may attempt a "clarification", which poor Eliot would see as obfuscation.

Here we go. The first few lines are quite straightforward even for the most inexperienced of us. As we grow older, we find that this "past", recorded by the bones on the beach, and so forth, no longer looks like mere sequence—a pointless lineup, that is, of events, with nothing more than hap to account for the arrangement. Nor can it be said to be "development", as the evolutionists see it: this is to discard the past ("disown" is Eliot's word) as somehow less perfect than the present, since all you get in an evolutionary past are rudimentary forms that are supplanted by "higher" forms. It is worth noting, however, that Eliot qualifies his remarks on popular evolutionary notions by the phrase "a partial fallacy". It is fallacious to see the past merely pushing upward in this Darwinian manner. If you take that view, you can pat the past on the head, so to speak, and disown it as "primitive" and, in some sense, discard-able. This is what C. S. Lewis called "chronological snobbery", meaning if it's newer, it is *thereby* better. But there is, at the same time, a sense in which the past *does* adumbrate the future (which is our present, by the way). We may refer ourselves to the opening lines of "Burnt Norton" here.

This past seems to take on "another pattern", if we are following Eliot's line of thought. This pattern is glimpsed in the moments of "sudden illumination", such as the moment in the draughty church at smokefall, or the moment when the rain beat on the arbor. That is one form in which eternity seems to pierce the scrim of time briefly. Ordinary "moments of happiness" are not quite what Eliot is talking about. The sense of well-being, for example, which may suffuse us when we get a raise in salary or win the pole-vault event or are elected to the chair—or even enjoy a fancy dinner at La Grenouille—is perfectly legitimate, but it is not what Eliot is talking about.

No. It is those fugitive moments of illumination that reveal the hem of eternity's garment, as it were. We "had the experience", certainly, in the draughty church or the arbor, but we couldn't quite lay hold of what it *meant*. Insofar as we even approached the meaning, perhaps in recollection afterward, we found the experience "restored" in a form different from the dismal sequence recorded by the bone on the beach, or even from the upward-pushing energy of the evolutionists' past. And certainly it outstrips altogether "any meaning / We can assign to happiness". Bravo to happiness; but what Eliot is talking about is higher, or deeper (the way up and the way down), than anything mere happiness can hint at.

And, says Eliot, "I have said before" that the full weight of past experiences, which have disclosed their significance once we *have* grasped their meaning, turns out to be, not just my private hallucinations, or yours, but rather the experience "of many generations". The testimony issues from the whole race of us mortals. The "hints and guesses" that tease us in the moments of illumination *are indeed reliable*. They do, in fact, bespeak Reality, not illusion. The stab of ecstasy that reached the quick of our soul for one nanosecond in the draughty church at smokefall came, not from some illusionary region of our mere subconscious, but from "the region of the summer stars", so to speak. Eliot, in other words, is crediting these experiences with a validity that comes from regions of Reality that are both higher and deeper than the regions mapped by Freud and Jung and Sir James Fraser. We might as well face it: *Four Quartets* takes Joy as seriously as did *The Divine Comedy*, and Saint John's Apocalypse. Joy is the very property of Reality, and it is really, truly *there* in the sense expressed in the carol *In Dulci Jubilo*, whose lines culminate with "O, that we were there, O, that we were there."

For Eliot, the Christian believer, this "there" is not an

illusion: it is solid with a solidity next to which Everest is diaphanous.

But we must not forget something—"Something that is probably quite ineffable". What is it? Well, it is the thing that peers at us when we look back *behind* all the "certainties" of the history books; it is "the primitive terror". Hurrah for historical studies and archeology and paleontology and geology. But they scratch the surface only. What is behind, or beneath, or beyond what they offer us? Ah. The Big Bang? That is impressive enough. But beyond *that*? The curtains of Eternity, hanging like the aurora borealis over our heads from who knows what cosmic or, rather, celestial heights.

In the light of this immensity, we find out that the moments of agony, like the moments of ecstasy, "are likewise permanent". They pierce those curtains. It does not matter whether we ourselves were all muddled with misunderstandings or futile hopes and dreads: that does not much matter. We may recall here that Eliot has already adjured us to "wait without hope", if we wish to hold ourselves still as Reality discloses itself, perhaps with the stillness with which the Virgin received the Annunciation. But even if we cannot quite manage that, nevertheless the moments (of agony or ecstasy) are "permanent / With such permanence as time has". With such permanence as time has! How Eliotean. To dismiss, in a mere aside, all of our trust in *time*, which contains, we like to tell ourselves, all the permanence there is, surely? Well, this permanence is not very permanent in the light of the permanence of which Eliot (and Dante, and the carol) speaks. *That* permanence is so real that we can endure it only in the most fugitive hints, since "humankind cannot bear very much reality."

It is easier for us to grasp ("appreciate") this if we scrutinize the agony of others who are near enough to us to involve us in at least some of the force of their agony, rather than if we try to unscramble our own agonies. The trouble with these latter agonies is that they are all mixed in with "currents of action"—what we have done, or might have done, or wish we had done, and so forth and so forth. Whereas others' torments are *there* for our contemplation, "unqualified" by all the jumble that litters our own, and "unworn by subsequent attrition". They do not dwindle into the past, as our own torments do. We can contemplate the torment of Job, or the *agon* of Samson, in the present, as it were, since we encounter these *as* present. But it need not be as remote a business as Job's or Samson's. The people we know: they "change, and smile: but the agony abides". The smiles *succeed* the agony, but that is all they can do: succeed. They do not unmake the agony. The agony testifies to the reality of the Past, which, we will recall, Eliot has been speaking of since the first line of "Burnt Norton".

And now, "Time the destroyer is time the preserver." There's a truism for us all. But would we have thought of it? Poets think of things like this that stare us in the face all the time and that the rest of us brush past in our distraction. It is a truism, to be sure, but it is also a paradox. To make it dramatically plain, Eliot returns to his river. All the junk that the river has swept from its banks flows past us. And Eliot will not mince words: the "cargo" of the river is a cargo of "dead negroes, cows, and chicken coops". No doubt we all think of the Mississippi and its role in the American Civil War. But the Yangtse or the Volga or the Congo will do as well. There seem to be some apples among the wreckage, bitter—and there's one with a bite out of it.

You can't read about an apple with a bite out of it without thinking of Eve and the Fall. And that "apple" *was* bitter. All this cargo of tragedy and all the torment and agony of which we have been reading are the legacy of that sorry and disobedient bite. Eliot summons the whole vast drama by noting a bit of garbage.

And the water of this river is also, of course, the water that tosses over the rocks at sea off Cape Ann, or wherever, very dangerous because of the fog. On a sunshiny ("halcyon") day, at low tide, these rocks are a sort of monument. They even have a name: The Dry Salvages. You can navigate by them. But in fog or tempest, the nice rocks will kill you—as has always been the grim truth of the matter.

III

The first few lines in section III need a footnote, no question about that. Let us remember that the topic in section II has been the apparently hopeless business of trying to keep up with time ("forever bailing") and the inexorable way in which the past simply carries things away—with this qualification, namely, that there may be "another pattern", hinted at by "The moments of happiness" or, rather, the moments "beyond any meaning / We can assign to happiness", in which we seem to penetrate to a dimension behind mere "recorded history", which bespeaks a "permanence" not eroded by time.

It is against this backdrop that Krishna's remark seems apposite (although Eliot prefaces the whole thing with a demurral: "I sometimes wonder if that is what Krishna meant—"). Far be it from Eliot, especially in these vast precincts, to insist on a formula that will lay all of our questions to rest. In any event, it may help the reader if we point out that Krishna, in his exhortation to the warrior Arjuna, told Arjuna to acquire "disinterestedness". That is a word whose meaning has become twisted in our own time. It really means "detachment", that is, the refusal to invest situations and things with some outcome that I insist must follow my actions. Arjuna was a member of the ruling warrior class and had the duty to avenge the death of a kinsman. Krishna, the god, justifies the act by pointing out that Arjuna must fulfill his dharma (his appointed role, task, and destiny) in the bigger drama, since, when the chips are down, slayer and slain are at one in that neither can possibly comprehend the divine will. Hence, Arjuna must simply act, without calculating the fruits. All of this is found in the *Baghavad Gita*, with which Eliot was very familiar.

Eliot again demurs by adding "Among other things—or one way of putting the same thing". He prefers a tentative note here, rather than any note struck by pontificating. We are all out of our depth when it comes to this riddle of time and what we are supposed to do. We act in time (". . . bailing, / Setting and hauling", or biting into a disastrous apple), and the river floats it all away, refusing to distinguish between the dead negroes and the chicken coops. As far as mere *time* is concerned, ". . . the future is a faded song."

What's that? In the next few lines, Eliot reverses time's sequence, as it were, treating the future as though it were already the past, since in the implacable inevitability of time's movement, it seems to be a mere quibble as to whether any given act or choice or effort is in the past, the present, or the future, as it all has to happen anyway, and "time present and time future" become "time past", however furiously we set and haul and bail, or fulfill our dharma.

So. Let us try looking at the future, so full of possibility and expectation for us mortals, as though it were already past. A faded song: say, all the brisk songs written about World War I—"Over There" and "It's a Long Way to Tipperary" and "K-K-K-Katy". Those songs are now in the yellowed pile, all dog-eared, of sheet music in the attic, no matter what excitement attended their bursting upon the patriotic public and no matter what heroism, idealism, and poignance are invoked in their lyrics. Even "God Bless America": Who can even remotely recover the sheer *thrill* that ran up and down our spines as Kate Smith sang that to us over the radio during World War II?

It is likewise with this Royal Rose. The White Rose of York and the Red Rose of Lancaster, in the fifteenth-century Wars of the Roses in England, were flowers for which men died. But now? Well, there they are, in the past or, at best, in some heraldry that recalls that past. And the lavender spray: that lies in the drawer, the way the bowl of roses sits on the lady's parlor table, arousing "wistful regret"—"*for those who are not yet here to regret*" (italics mine). What? How can you regret the disappearance of people who haven't even been born yet (which implies that you, the regretter, aren't either). Well, Eliot is violently telescoping past, present, and future. Poetry is nothing if it does not *vivify* for us the commonplaces, which we all treat as commonplaces but which are in reality thunderbolts from Ultimacy, so to speak. I muddle along through time, encountering this event and that regret, hardly ever flagged down with the thought that "my" experience has already been run and rerun for generations and millennia, until there are no treads at all left on the wheels. The leaves in the memory scrapbook "that has never been opened" are already yellow in this time warp with which Eliot is regaling us.

So, what escape is there from this melancholy drainage? Eliot is not interested in any mere escape. He is interested, in the *Quartets*, in the solid Reality that catches ("contains"— back to the opening lines of "Burnt Norton") the drainage.

"And the way up is the way down, the way forward is the

way back." Nostalgia won't recover the past; and high idealism won't guarantee the future; and the present is caught in
the interstice, if we will insist on squinting at mere sequence.
But if we will open our eyes and resolve to press on through
"this turning world", we might be vouchsafed a glimpse of
the Still Point "where past and future are gathered".

We "cannot face it steadily", of course: "human kind /
Cannot bear very much reality." We have to come at it by a
thousand ruses, or say, rather, by paying attention to the
"hints and guesses" that are forever at our elbows. Certainly
"time is no healer". It merely carries everything away. The
patient, once so hopeful of recovery, "is no longer here".
Time, that is to say Death, has taken him offstage.

Eliot here offers two cases in point from the ordinary life of
Everyman that might help us catch the force of all that he is
saying. (I say "the ordinary life": it *was* ordinary back in 1940,
when Eliot was writing. Nowadays very few people travel
either on trains or on ocean liners. But we can follow him,
nevertheless.)

The train pulls out, the passengers settle ("To fruit, peri-
odicals and business letters": poetry is nothing if it is not
concrete), the people who waved them off have left the plat-
form, the passengers' faces relax now (they may have wept a
bit at the parting), and the clickety-click on the rails lulls
them all. They are not, however, "escaping" the past: the
stark fact is that they are not the same people who left the
station, nor are they the same people who will arrive at
the destination. *Time*, with its past (at the station), present
(here in the compartment), and future (at the destination),
does its work. We mortals cannot surmount it. We change.

It is thus with an ocean voyage. Few modern readers will
have had the experience of standing at the taffrail, watching
the great wide wake of the steamer stretching back to the

horizon. It was a mesmeric experience, believe me. But thoughts that are lashed to time won't suffice ("the past is finished" or "the future is before us"). The wind's voice in the rigging, like the tolling bell of the buoy, "Measures time not our time . . . a time / Older than the time of chronometers". It comes from farther away than the coils of the conch shell that whisper in your ear, and no mortal language can speak it. The message here is "Fare forward, you who think you are voyaging." Like the passengers in the train, you are not the same people who left the harbor, nor are you the ones who will disembark at Southampton, Bombay, or Singapore. Out here on the Atlantic, "while time is withdrawn" (back to the moment when you set sail), put your mind to it: "consider the future / And the past with an equal mind". Try, that is, to gain the perspective to which the entirety of the *Quartets* summons us, in which past, present, and future are all "contained" in each other, and from which perspective alone you may, sooner or later, see the "pattern" of all the contingencies, "reconciled among the stars".

The thing is, it is "At the moment which is not of action or inaction" that we are best placed to "receive this". The passengers on the train or the liner, for example, cannot be said to be "active" (they are settled in the compartment or standing at the rail) or "inactive" (they are moving through both space and time). But if they will only be attentive to this paradoxical situation in which they find themselves, they will be especially well placed to "receive this"—the following remark, that is, which is certainly dire: "on whatever sphere of being / The mind of a man may be intent / At the time of death" is the one action that has the particular property of authenticity, namely, that it will "fructify in the lives of others".

We need a bit of help here. The thing is too freighted with

meaning. Well, then, first: that point about what we are intent on at the moment of death—why that? Catholic theology sees almost inifinite significance in the *articulo mortis*—the moment of death. It is not so much that our eternal well-being stands or falls absolutely with the hair-trigger possibilities of what we may have our minds on at that moment. The chances are that at that moment we might well be in a coma, or thinking, "Help! That great lorry is going to run me down!" or other such hasty alarms. No: the situation is rather that the state of mind "at the still point of the turning world", to which Eliot has been courteously but inexorably summoning us since the opening lines, is a state detached from the *mere* sequence of past, present, and future; or say, rather, that it is the state of the soul that, having seen the futility of one's being "distracted from distraction by distraction", is poised on the cusp between the conditioned ("this twittering world") and the Unconditioned ("the darkness", say) and is, thereby, prepared truly to "Fare forward".

This attitude partakes of the nature of *Caritas* (the divine Charity), which Eliot has not yet mentioned, but which is certainly the rubric governing our true "end". Only this, which is the mark of the saints, will "fructify in the lives of others". My life for yours: it is the principle of Charity and is virtually synonymous with salvation. Hell, the dead end, loathes this: paradise dances to this choreography.

But we have omitted Eliot's parenthesis: "(And the time of death is every moment)". The whole poem has been trumpeting this at us. If my moments are simply whirled by the turning world, then I am ready for nothing. I am like the "Men and bits of paper, whirled by the cold wind / That blows before and after time". My "End" will come upon me as calamity. But if, like the saints, I locate my being at, or at least as near as possible to, the Still Point, then when at death the "turning" suddenly ceases, I will already be familiar with the precincts. And, returning to Krishna's advice to Arjuna, I must not be obsessed with "the fruit of action", anxiously weighing this, that, or the other option with an eye on the possible results. I must simply act, or refrain from action, in obedience to the choreography appointed me from the Still Point, where the dance is (and, I may recall to my soul's salvation, "there is only the dance").

So. "Fare forward." The ordinary parting remark is "Fare-well." But, since that has slid into virtual meaninglessness (it only means "good-bye" to most of us), Eliot, the poet, must awaken us by a slightly alternative injunction. *Fare forward.* Don't be merely whirled about or distracted. Make your journey, not merely from Victoria Station to Tilbury on British Rail, or to Bombay on P&O Orient Lines, but to your End. This is our real destination. Whether we *arrive* at either of those *mere* "destinations" or whether we drown en route, "Or whatever event", is not finally of much importance. So Krishna told Arjuna: the outcome of the fight is neither here nor there. Do what you must do.

A small warning flag might be apposite here. Readers might be forgiven for concluding that Eliot is recommending an entirely fatalistic outlook here: no choice, act, or result matters. Dharma is all. I think, however, that from Eliot's Christian point of view, dharma would be a limited, and depressing, notion. Certainly there is the inexorable summons to us all to Fare forward, regardless. But there is nothing blind or impersonal or superpersonal about it. *My* destiny, in the End, will turn out to be synonymous with the glorious individual who is me. There is no trace of mere absorption into the Whole in the Christian Eliot. His point of view is that of John of the Cross and the Lady Julian of Norwich. The End does not obliterate *me*: it will disclose the real and glorious me, who alone, in my fullest individuality, can dance the steps awaiting me in the Dance.

IV

And now the lyric. It is a prayer to our Lady. Protestant and non-religious readers may be reminded here that Catholic piety characteristically addresses petitions to the Virgin, not by way of circumventing Christ, our High Priest, but rather by way of recognizing that she, along with all others in the Christian fold, is given a share in that priestly office of intercession. The Body does what the Head does. To ask the Virgin for her intercession is indistinguishable from asking Tom, Dick, or Harry for his prayers—except, of course, that her prayers will certainly be purified from all tincture of self-interest or distraction. If it is objected that she is "up there" in heaven and can't hear us, we may recall that Catholics believe that the Resurrection of our Lord overleaped the hitherto insurmountable barrier of Death and that the Church in Pilgrimage (us on earth) and the Church Triumphant (those in paradise) are one, living, undivided, interceding Body. (It is also worth noting here that there is no syllable of all this defensive and laborious explication in Eliot. He is making poetry, not apologetics.)

So we address the "Lady, whose shrine stands on the promontory". Ships come to grief on the rocks at the base of promontories. Hence the particular aptness of this shrine as the *métier* for our prayers in behalf of all voyagers. We need no help with the list that follows of those for whom we pray, except possibly to point out yet again the "dryness" of Eliot's poetry: "those / Whose business has to do with fish. . . ." Very humdrum stuff, very far from any "periphrastic study in

a worn-out poetical fashion". These men in the fishing in-
dustry are very much like the passengers settling down to
fruit and business letters. Here also are our "anxious worried
women / Lying awake", wondering if their sons and hus-
bands will ever return.

Figlia del tuo figlio. Daughter of your Son. Dante, whom
Eliot quotes here, caught the mystery of the Incarnation
in four words. A most potent invocation here. "Queen of
Heaven": again, non-Catholic readers may set aside their
fears lest the Church has erected another Astarte next to the
King of Heaven. We are all, says Saint Paul, destined to be
crowned with glory; and the figure of the Virgin thus
crowned is the archetype of this glorification that is the destiny of all men who will take the Way up or the Way down.

We also pray for the dead: all who *were* sailing, but who
were wrecked on the sand or drowned in the "dark throat" of
the Maelstrom, say—or, for that matter, any and all, wherever
they may have ended up, who cannot hear "the sound of the
sea bell's / Perpetual angelus".

What's that? The bell, of course, is the buoy, warning
mariners about the promontory. The "angelus" is the prayer
repeated by Catholics, both Roman and Anglo-, thrice daily,
which rehearses the Annunciation, with the Virgin's re-
sponses, most notably her "Be it done unto me according to
thy word." Only insofar as I join my own prayer to the
angelus will I be saved from the dark throat, the sand, or the
shoals.

V

I have never been able to make up my mind whether Eliot
wrote the opening fifteen lines of this section (down to

". . . the Edgeware Road") with especial relish—even, perhaps, a certain naughty glee. The point is, it *is* funny, although at the end of the day, of course, the subject is fathomlessly serious.

What we have here is a dismal roster of the tactics, fatuous in the extreme, pursued by the modern world by way of "getting in touch", shall we say, with—with what? Well, with destiny, or Whatever-is-*There*, or what's coming. What these tactics all come down to is the effort to poke through the scrim that hangs between the seen and the unseen, or between our mortal life and the transcendence that bedevils us all. The tactics are fatuous if *Four Quartets* is a true accounting of things, since in the scheme of things bespoken in this poem there is no shortcut at all to our true destiny. We will find, later in this same section, that there is nothing for it but "prayer, observance, discipline, thought and action". You can't pop in to a palmist or Tarot reader and come at the truth.

Once again, readers will for the most part be able to make their own way along in these lines. We come upon astrology first, then séances, then whatever it is that people do about the sea serpent, then, after our horoscope, we run into Eliotean territory. To haruspicate is to rummage through sheeps' entrails in order to discover whether you, if you are Caesar, are going to win the battle against the Goths. They did this in Rome and other ancient royal capitals. "Scry" is a form of "descry", which means to peer into things, as it were. Graphoanalysis, palmistry, sortilege (casting lots, etc.), tea leaves, the Tarot cards, the pentagram (frequently thought to be a figure that will yield up various secrets), and LSD, which, readers will recall either from hearsay or from their own sorties, suffuses one with the impression that one has arrived in the precincts of clarity. Then we have psychoanalysis (Freud) and Jung, and even the Great Pyramid, which greatly excited everyone when it was opened, the idea being that it contained vast secrets that might well throw light on things.

But the payoff is Eliot's weary and Olympian dismissal of the entire enterprise, as though it is of no more significance (which it isn't) than all the other "usual / Pastimes . . . and features of the press", along with the comics, the fashion and food sections, and the op eds.

You get people hurrying to these purlieus "When there is distress of nations and perplexity / Whether on the shores of Asia, or in the Edgeware Road". Whether it is war threatening in the Pacific in 1941 or my own anxieties in my flat here in the Edgeware Road makes no difference. Anxiety is anxiety, and we want to get *in touch* somehow. And besides, we mortals are always curious about the distant past, and certainly about the future.

But. And here we must altogether admit that there is no possible way of stating the thing other than what we find in Eliot's lines (which, of course, is starkly true of the entirety of the *Quartets* and, Eliot would insist, of all poetry worthy of the name): ". . . to apprehend / The point of intersection of the timeless / With time, is an occupation for the saint—". The acidhead, the medium, the card reader, and the psychoanalyst will never arrive at this point so long as they trust their own tactics. We have already admitted, but it is worth repeating ("You say I am repeating / Something I have said before. I shall say it again. / Shall I say it again?"): *Four Quartets* is about sanctity, that is, the Way (up or down) by which we mortals may finally win through to the Beatific Vision. No other "reading" of the poem will do justice to Eliot's work here. Anything but the blunt Catholic reading of the thing is mere whistling in the dark.

The saint's "occupation" is not, we find, like other jobs one finds to do—the work of the bank clerk, the plumber, or the vice president for community relations. It is, rather, an operation of grace: "something given / And taken, in a lifetime's death in love, / Ardour and selflessness and self-surrender". There is no other way. "If any man will come after me, let him deny himself, take up his cross, and follow me." Those are the marching orders, and there are no short-cuts or platinum card privileges. Beatitude will not cast its pearls before swine. Who shall ascend . . . ?

In the next seven lines, we find that "For most of us" the thing catches our attention at best only in fugitive moments, scarcely noted by us. This "point of intersection of the time-less / With time" flashes on our attention like one single flash of a strobe light, gone before we collect ourselves. This "distraction fit" may evoke fleetingly for us the scent of wild thyme, straight out of *A Midsummer Night's Dream*, a region that we would give our souls to visit. Or, here we have it again, the "unheard music", that is, the insupportable music that is only faintly evoked by, say, a Mozart horn concerto. The intensity of this kind of experience, fleeting though it may be, is such that any disjuncture between "me" and "the music" disappears. All is one seamless, blissful fabric.

But again. "These are only hints and guesses." This certainly must be grasped as a phrase crucial to the whole of the *Quartets*. The experience is, actually, *true*, in the sense that what is glimpsed is, in fact, the hem of the garment of Beatitude. These fleeting moments are not illusionary. We have been stricken with the dart of *sehnsucht*, the inconsolable longing for That Which is, so far, unimaginable to us.

I have often thought that what might be glimpsed in seri-ous astrology or in sortilege or even LSD might well be a glimpse of something that is true at the center of things. The error lies not so much in the glimpse as in my *fixing upon* the glimpse as in some way salvific. The point is, hints and guesses are only hints and guesses. Flags. But to get *there* is the occupation for the saint. I cannot suddenly land there by popping a pill.

". . . and the rest / Is prayer, observance, discipline, thought and action". There is the bald truth. There is no shortcut. It is lifetime's death in love.

The truth of the matter, which has been hinted at and guessed and half understood, "is Incarnation".

Oh. A hasty reader might wish Eliot had said *the* Incarnation. And of course, by capitalizing the word, he has bundled us all, Christian or non-Christian, Catholic or non-Catholic, right along to the single point where we find ourselves hailed by the Incarnation of the Word. But his poetry is not ready for this pat business yet. What is hinted and guessed at is the whole mystery of incarnation, namely, the incorrigible habit of all things to come to a point (everything that rises must converge), that point being *flesh*. *The* Word was incarnate by the Holy Ghost of the Virgin Mary because that is what the Word *does*. From before the Creation, this was in the cards (to put it frivolously). But given the reticence so characteristic of Eliot and of his poetry, we don't want to land bang in the *Bible* quite yet (and we never do, actually, at least in Eliot). Poetry draws the thread out, so to speak, to an infinitely finer thinness than does preaching. Or, to bring into play the Dance, which we have already encountered, poetry dances *on point*, whereas preaching stumps along earnestly.

Now we lay hold in very truth of the thing we strained at in our fatuous recourse to sortilege and tea leaves, namely, "the impossible union / Of spheres of existence". Here, and here alone, we find earth and heaven to be one. Flesh and fleshless. Time and eternity. Contingency and ultimacy. So—past and future, far from being unredeemable (see "Burnt

Norton", line 5), are not only appeased: they are "conquered and reconciled".

Eliot is uttering, in these short, quiet lines of poesy, matters that brood over and animate all wars, loves, yearnings, enterprises, art, music, building, generating, plowing and reaping, mending, and everything else that pertains to our identity as human. All of the action entailed in those items is only "movement / Of that which is only moved / And it has no source of movement". Insofar as those efforts spring only from *our* resources, they belong to the twittering world. They are "only moved", like the men and bits of paper whirled by the cold wind. They have found no center. All is haywire. All is Babel. Or Babylon, over which will be trumpeted one fine day, "Babylon the great is fallen, is fallen." Its denizens are "Driven by daemonic, chthonic / Powers". A splendid Eliotean word meaning "of the earth". On the other hand, "right action" follows upon, or leads to, our release "From past and future also". Again we are back to the opening five lines of "Burnt Norton", which articulate, in lapidary fashion, the problem.

The final nine lines of "The Dry Salvages" call for little assistance from any commentator, except perhaps the remark that "our temporal reversion" refers to our death and decomposition—our reverting to the earth because we are creatures in time—which will help fertilize the soil, which is "significant" in that it bears the whole record, under the species of time, of our story. And (in a penultimate parenthesis) we hope we have the good fortune to be buried in the churchyard (near the Still Point, that is), which is where we find the yew-tree.

Little Gidding

I

We are nearing the place toward which the entire poem has been straining. Little Gidding, readers will recall, is the place where in the seventeenth century one Nicholas Ferrar attempted to establish a lay community that would, as much as possible, organize its daily activities around the Eucharist and the canonical hours. Obviously they could not ask people to arise every three hours during the night, as was the case in monasteries, for matins, lauds, prime, and so forth. But surely it must be possible for us mortals to live plain lay life in *some* sort of recognition of, and obedience to, the choreography the liturgy imposes on time. Little Gidding, then, would present the opportunity for families and other laymen to live in a proximity as close as is possible under the species of time and our mortal flesh, to the Still Point, since in the tabernacle on the altar in the chapel there would be the Blessed Sacrament, which is the flesh that stands on the cusp between time and eternity, or between the imperfections of our ordinary lives and Beatitude.

What is this "Midwinter spring" that opens the section? It may be like the late November disturbed by spring in "East Coker"—a sort of time-out-of-time, or time unhinged from the normal expectations of the calendar. A sudden warm flush in the middle of winter calls into question such expectations. But this "spring is its own season / Sempiternal . . ." How so (sempiternal means "enduring constantly or continually;

everlasting")? Well, if it defies the calendar, say, then perhaps it partakes of a quality unavailable to mere time. I myself would not insist on this understanding of the situation, but it is at least one possible reading of the cryptic lines. If I am right, then of course the rest follows. At Little Gidding one finds time punctuated (or defied) by eternity. The altar is a case in point of such a punctuation; and here we have this odd weather, which, given the point of view at work in this community, might be perceived as another case in point of this punctuation of time by eternity. In the rest of England people would simply say, "A bit of a warm spell, eh?" and leave it at that. But at Little Gidding, time has been opened up to eternity, or the quotidian opened to the unconditioned, say.

But because it *is*, in fact, just a meteorological phenomenon, it is subject to the covenant that governs weather. The ice has melted briefly and unseasonably, so things get soggy toward evening. The moment seems "Suspended" between the pole (winter) and the tropics (hot weather).

The next seventeen lines work this theme of winter and spring, cold and heat, and, most notably, ice and fire. We may recall here "East Coker", II, and the "vortex that shall bring / The world to that destructive fire / Which burns before the ice-cap reigns". Eliot is drawing on the old commonplace that ice is to be found beyond the fire of apocalypse. The *locus classicus* here is, of course, Dante's hell, where we find Lucifer at the bottom of hell, far below the flames and burning sand, up to his waist in ice, and everything down there shaggy with ice.

Here at Little Gidding, at the brightest part of the day, it seems as though we have both frost and fire simultaneously, with the sun flaming on the ice of ponds and ditches with a glare that blinds us. But what is this "windless cold that is the heart's heat"? This seems odd—a non sequitur, really. Well, we find out presently. This fiery chill turns out to be "pentecostal fire", which, like that original Pentecostal fire, "Stirs the dumb spirit". "Dumb" here implies mute, not stupid. The whole interlude partakes of the stillness that may attend the arrivals of the Holy Spirit, as in the "still, small voice" heard by Elijah, rather than in the sound of rushing wind at the original Pentecost.

The life of our souls ("the soul's sap") *always* quivers "Between melting and freezing". The trembling insubstantiality of our mortality is always beset, on the one hand, by fire (here I think it is the fire of the divine Love) and ice (perdition). The choice is always ours. This uncovenanted spring time yields none of the rich smells that hail us with the rise of real spring. The hedges are blanched with snow and not the hawthorn that sprinkles all English hedgerows in spring. The snow itself is, of course, "transitory" (like our souls), since sooner or later it will melt, but right now its bloom seems more striking even than summer's blossoms. The hedgerow here neither buds nor fades, since it is held, as it were, in the motionlessness of winter. This whole odd reminder of summer, however, is "Not in the scheme of generation". What scheme is that? The scheme visible in "the living seasons / The time of the seasons and the constellations / The time of milking and the time of harvest / The time of the coupling of man and woman . . ." ("East Coker", I). No generating is going on here. It is just "Sudden in a shaft of sunlight . . ." ("Burnt Norton", V).

But then where is the real, eternal, vivifying summer of unimaginable beauty, of which this midwinter spring is merely a fleeting epiphany? We yearn for the "Zero" summer, that is, the state of affairs at the Still Point, which is not to be quantified. Where is it? Of what bliss is this a hint or guess?

The people at Little Gidding, unlike the drooping souls in the Underground, and those distracted from distraction by distraction, and the distinguished civil servants and chairmen of many committees, are keenly alive to the intersection of the timeless with time. For them, all is redolent of hints and guesses.

Visitors to Little Gidding, from wherever they may have come, will find things unexceptionable. In May, for example, the hawthorn will be intensely sweet, unlike the ephemeral "blossoms" of snow that deck the hedges in winter. Whether they are pilgrims, or chance tourists, or somebody like a broken king (Charles I, who very much liked Little Gidding, and who was certainly "broken" by Cromwell?), they will have to make their way along the rough road and past the pig-sty if they want to arrive at the Still Point, which is here. This journey is not unlike the journey every man must make, whether he is a king or a thrall. Everyone, no matter what his station in life, is going to be greatly surprised at how the actual arrival outstrips all of their notions as to what they would find here. Casual tourists will be haled up from their various distractions, and even serious pilgrims are going to find that their expectations are supervened by the reality of the place. Only the fulfillment will reveal what anyone's "purpose" should have been. In these precincts alone is to be found that fulfillment, since Little Gidding is, at least for Eliot's purpose in this poem, as close as we can get in this mortal life to the Still Point. Burnt Norton reminded us of how time can wholly obliterate things. East Coker, still a reminder of the past, also reminds us that "Home is where one starts from"—to go where? The Dry Salvages will either wreck you or assist you to "Fare forward".

Of course there are other final destinations: drowning, being shot down over a dark lake, parching in the desert, or whatever. But Little Gidding "is the nearest, in place and time, / Now and in England". This "Now and in England" will serve well enough to remind us that *all* "nows" have the potentiality to be "the nearest", and any geographical location will serve as the approach to the Still Point. It is just that Eliot has brought us to Little Gidding, which, because of its very nature, is a particularly explicit and stark approach.

A peculiar demand, or actually a prohibition, presides over this place, because it is a most holy (that is, purposefully set apart) place. You are going to have to divest yourself of "Sense and notion". You can't come here driven by appetency (see "Burnt Norton", III), that is, with your sensual faculties humming with busy desires, or by "notion"—all of your busy presuppositions in high gear. The language in the following lines could not be more elementary. They need not be re-worded here. We had better kneel.

Prayer pierces the scrim between time and the timeless, through to the region where the dead are to be found. They alone speak with the fiery tongues needed to bespeak the thunderous mystery and glory that looms over Little Gidding. Some language "beyond the language of the living" is necessary, like the Pentecostal tongues with which the apostles announced that glory. Insofar as we happen to be at Little Gidding, "the intersection of the timeless moment" happens to be in England. But no "where" can quite be imposed on this intersection, any more than any time ("Never and always"). At Little Gidding we find, as the shepherds found at the manger in Bethlehem, or the disciples at the Transfiguration, say, or wherever Love in its glory is glimpsed, a particularly stark epiphany of "what the dead had no speech for, when living".

Eliot, of course, was still one of the "living" when he wrote the poem. Hence, despite his titanic effort with words in the *Four Quartets*, he acknowledges that no words (speech) will quite suffice. This intersection of the timeless moment will yield its secrets only in the fulfillment. Dante himself would dismiss his *Paradiso* as so much chat in comparison with the glory into which one stumbles upon entering the Celestial Rose.

II

Eliot gives us rhymed couplets in this section. But the meter is irregular. The juxtaposition of rhyme and *irregular* meter prevents our being lulled, for one thing (we had better not be lulled, since the topic is death), and, for another, it is itself a case in point of the unpredictability that is perhaps death's most unnerving characteristic.

We get death under the four aspects of the four elements. In other words, there will be no escaping death, because it pervades the whole of created reality.

It is all very bleak. For instance, the roses, with all the memories they evoke of young love and fragrant beauty, leave only ash behind, and this ash is no more impressive than the droppings of the old man's cigar. Ashes to ashes. Roses or cigars. It all comes to the same thing in the end. And the smallest movement of air can scatter them. They are insubstantial in the extreme. Or dust. The climax of a whole story, when the telling is over, even if it is *The Iliad*, leaves only dust in the air. And this house that has gone to ruin, with the very walls and wainscots, and even the mouse who trotted there: the whole business leaves only this dusty detritus. Neither the hope, which looked for some way to avoid the ruin, nor the despair, which assumed the ruin, makes much difference in the end. It all comes to the same thing.

Or, you can have a flood swamping the earth, or a drought parching the earth. Neither state of affairs encourages life, shall we say. You can be drowned in the one or find yourself buried in sand (if you are trying to walk across the Sahara). The outcome is the same. The soil, in the latter case, being "eviscerate" (with all of the life leeched out of it), simply stares stolidly at your efforts to plow it or dig it or shape it. It mocks us.

Or you can have a town, or a pasture, or just a patch of weeds: sooner or later water or fire will obliterate all. These two elements, in their turn, mock "the sacrifice that we denied". How do we parse that? Well, the water or fire will obliterate both the things we have willingly given up and the things we clung to for dear life in a tragicomic effort to keep them intact. Resist ("deny") as we will, everything will be torn from our grasp sooner or later. And the elements will rot the ancient foundations of the cathedral, with its sanctuary and choir up beyond the transept, so splendid in their day.

Now we come to a most peculiar scene. A great deal of speculation has been expended on these lines. As we have pointed out more than once, Eliot would cordially demur if we were to tax him for an exact "interpretation". Our question would be wrong. Insofar as his poetry can be read only by imposing an interpretative grid on it, then he will have failed, he would urge.

Having said that, we have no option, if we are going to say anything at all, but to do the very thing he would object to, always insisting loudly that our effort is a *pis aller*. The elaboration that follows is to be firmly set aside once it has served its modest, and admittedly awkward, purpose of suggesting one possible toehold in the poetry. I might also add that I have not cobbled up on my own what follows. I first encountered this reading of things in a graduate class at New York

University under Oscar Cargill, an Eliot scholar of venerable memory.

The scene may, at least on one level, be taken to be the rubble of London in the early morning during the blitz in 1940, just after the German bombers have headed back across the North Sea to their own airfields in Germany. Eliot did, in fact, serve as what we in America called an air-raid warden. These were layman, as opposed to military, who wore tin helmets and who reported fires and assisted the citizens. Of course, the night of bombing has seemed "interminable", and the whole ghastly business is "recurrent" and also "unending", both in the sense that it occurs night after night, and also that, on any given night, wave after wave of bombers unload their destruction, while one wonders if there is no end of Germany's supply of bombers. They are accompanied by smaller Messerschmidts and Stukas, like dark doves, with their outspread wings black against the night sky, and their "tongues" flickering with machine-gun fire as the R.A.F. fighters ascend to engage them. Eliot was perfectly aware that no one can read of doves and flickering tongues without thinking of the Holy Spirit, traditionally pictured as a dove, descending with tongues of flame upon the apostles gathered in the room. But surely this would be a sacrilegious layering of meanings? Not in Eliotean terms, since both the bombers and the Holy Spirit do, in fact, bring ordinary expectations and routine life to a calamitous end, leaving us with the smoking residue of those routines and charging us with a dramatically altered vista. It was thus, we may also remark, when the Holy Spirit came upon the Blessed Virgin: that was the sudden devastation of her whole notion as to what her life was, and was to be.

The morning is quiet, except for the rattling of dead leaves over the asphalt. These leaves, of course, may be either literal leaves from blasted trees in Green Park or flakes and shards of tin blown from cars and buildings. The three smoking districts, we may suppose, are three sections of London—say, Westminster, Mayfair, and Saint James's—although more probably they would be districts far to the east of the West End, in the docklands, which suffered the heaviest bombing.

Readers will have noticed that we have had not so much as a comma for the last eight lines. The punctuation, or absence thereof, underscores the unreal, almost nightmare, nature of the scene, since all is run together in one undifferentiated region of ruin. The poet (or warden), dazed by the blitz, can scarcely punctuate one impression from another.

Presently a figure appears, whether loitering or hurrying is far from clear in this general blur. We suspect that it may be a ghost, since it is being blown along like the leaves. The warden scrutinizes the down-turned face and supposes that he has "caught the sudden look of some dead master / Whom I had known, forgotten, half recalled . . ." The "brown baked features", like the features of a desiccated corpse several centuries old—the sort of thing you see in glass coffins under the altars in European churches—have a peculiar property: they seem to be the face(s) of "one and many"—a "compound ghost" whom the warden (or let us just say the poet) seems both to know and not to know. Whoever it (or they) may be, it appears to be "some dead master". Dante? Homer? Virgil? Eliot would insist (see his essay "Tradition and Individual Talent") that any poet owes unpayable debts to these gentlemen.

Our poet, unsure whether he knows the figure or not, assumes a double part, namely, that of a new acquaintance and of an old pupil. The cry "What! are *you* here?" breaks the silence, but it is not clear which of them has spoken. Or did they speak simultaneously? It doesn't matter. Yet the cry

coming from the strange figure is enough to satisfy our poet
that he does, now, recognize who it is. Let us say, for better or
worse, that it is Dante. They join each other, walking together "in a dead patrol". The active patrol of the warden has
been absorbed into this visionary patrol, in and out of time,
and quite without reference to London's geography ("no-
where, no before and after"). Once again, as is always the case
with these "intersections" of time (with the timeless, as in the
garden in "Burnt Norton" and at Little Gidding), the very
strangeness of the whole ambience itself excludes any mistake
("Too strange to each other for misunderstanding"). That is
the way with the particular pressure and intensity that attend
these moments. Despite the strangeness, there is a "concord"
that presides over the thing.

Our poet wonders at two things: first, his sense of wonder,
and second, the ease that he immediately feels in the presence
of this dead master. An odd conversation follows.

The figure speaks of both his own work and that of our
poet, and the message seems to be that the poetry may be cast
aside. What? Surely if there is anything immortal in our poor
history, it would be the poetry of a Dante? Surely we must at
all costs preserve, and honor, the *Divina Commedia* (or *The
Iliad*, or *The Aeneid*)? No. "These things have served their
purpose: let them be." You mean that even *poetry* is expendable? Yes. It is only the voice. The Word is the lasting substance that the poetry only strains at, with shabby equipment
always deteriorating, and words that won't stay in place and
that slip, slide, and perish. So discouraging.

But that is not all. Not only is the poetry expendable. Far
from viewing your own poetry as some sort of cockade that
merits you the esteem of men, *you must pray for forgiveness for
this, your best effort*. Eheu! Surely . . . ?

No. That is the long and the short of it. *Nothing* that we do can suffice for the order of things that we encounter at the intersection, that is, the Still Point. In the order of time, the fruit of last season has been eaten. The epics of Homer and Virgil, and the *Commedia* itself, "have served their purpose". The pail is empty, to be kicked over by the cow. And you (Eliot, shall we say) have the daunting task of trying to say what we said, with the words that belong to your own time, fully realizing that your words, like mine (Dante, say), will also deteriorate and perish. "And next year's words await another voice."

Dante—let us just settle for Dante for the moment, knowing full well that the speaking voice is the voice of Poetry— goes on to say something like the following: The "passage" between the world where I am now (Purgatory, in Eliot's catholic vision) and your world clearly presents no hindrance, since I seem to be here. My spirit, so far, is "unappeased", that is, not yet satisfied, since the only ultimate satisfaction for anyone's spirit is the Beatific Vision, and I am far from having arrived. Hence, my spirit is also "peregrine"—a pilgrim, en route to that beatitude. The two worlds, namely, the world of my purgation and your world here at war, have an odd resemblance to each other. Each, that is, is the arena in which souls are being formed by suffering.

So, says Dante, I find myself saying things I never thought I'd have the chance to say. I am talking to a poet who is working six and a half centuries after my death. And I also find myself in streets I never thought I should visit when I left my body in Ravenna, on the shores of the Adriatic, having been exiled from my beloved Florence. Readers will note that I have not quoted Dante correctly. He says "*Revisit*". How can that be, since Dante never got as far afield as London? I think that the prefix intimates, for the hundredth time in the *Quartets*, the notion that time and place are inoperative in the state of affairs at the point of intersection (and Purgatory is certainly in the very near precincts of that point). So—Florence or London: both present city streets; either will do for what I am saying to you, my dear Eliot.

This may be the place for me to admit to something that attentive readers will long since have noticed. I have been calling the writer of the lines in the poem "Eliot" or "our poet", whereas I should, strictly, have been calling that writer "the persona". I am aware of this convention of scholarship, but it seems pedantic to insist on this convention in this stratospheric milieu. I would not quibble over the point, however.

Then Dante comes out with perhaps one of the most titanic lines ever spoken about poetry. He says that the great concern of us poets whose material is "speech" has been "To purify the dialect of the tribe / And urge the mind to aftersight and foresight".

There is a set of daunting marching orders for the poets. Contrary to popular misconception, poetry, far from being a bedecking of language, is a forcing of language through a purifying crucible under the most extreme rigors. In fact, Eliot has Dante say something even more drastic than that: language itself requires this fierce treatment if it is not to turn to mere dross. Language, in other words, *depends* on the poets. If we think this is fanciful, we may ask ourselves where the English language would be without Chaucer, Shakespeare, Milton, and Wordsworth. The trouble here is, of course, that poetry has faded altogether from the popular mind, and the language is now in a state of anarchy, where English-speaking people can say "I'm like" when they mean "I said". Dante (or Eliot) has been ignored, to our own impoverishment.

Furthermore, poetry obliges us to cope with both past ("aftersight") and future ("foresight"), not merely in the sense of its conjuring the past in its subject matter—the Trojan War, say, or Arthur—but, more important, by its compression of language, analogous to the compressing of past, present, and future at the Still Point.

With only a comma intervening, we find ourselves hailed with "the gifts reserved for age". We will recall that in "East Coker" we find the poet requesting, rather tartly perhaps, "Do not let me hear / Of the wisdom of old men, but rather of their folly . . ." Likewise here, when we are prepared to hear of the sagacity, venerability, and dignity that will crown our latter years, we find ourselves jarred by "the gifts reserved for age". They appear in sad contrast to the gold, frankincense, and myrrh offered once to an Infant.

Readers will scarcely need any comment on the first two gifts. But the third one might bear a remark. The heaviest burden of old age is the awful burden of penitence. The list is bleak. Read it. The most painful sting here, surely, is the realization that we shall discover that the very things "Which once you took for exercise of virtue" deserve only our shame.

This is a very unsparing section of "Little Gidding". If Dante and Eliot are going to have to beg forgiveness for their noblest achievements, where does that leave the rest of us, with our poor "virtues"? *Kyrie, eleison*, certainly, is the most earnest supplication that goes up from Purgatory. The prospect for us, upon realizing that all the approval in which we luxuriated was only the approval of fools, and the honors we amassed only a staining of the record, would be a grim and exasperating descent "From wrong to wrong . . . *unless restored by that refining fire*" (italics mine). Here is the fire again. Will it be the fire of hell or of the scorching Love of God? If it is the latter, we shall be enabled to enter the Dance.

That is the end of Dante's discourse. Day is breaking over the London rubble. Dante departs with a valediction, "And faded on the blowing of the horn", as Hamlet *pere's* ghost "faded on the crowing of the cock".

III

The third movement carries us a very long way forward from the grim states of affairs we find in the foregoing three books. In "Burnt Norton" we had the "time-ridden faces / Distracted from distraction by distraction", culminating, however, in the invitation to "Descend lower" to the "Internal darkness". A hint of salvation. In "East Coker" it was "O dark dark dark", with all those imposing men landing in "Nobody's funeral", but again the invitation to salvation with "I said to my soul, be still, and wait without hope. . . . So the darkness shall be the light, and the stillness the dancing." In "The Dry Salvages" we move from mere "wistful regret" to the injunction to "Fare forward. . . . Not fare well, But fare forward, voyagers." Again, some hint of the way up. "Little Gidding" brings us all the way.

We begin with a description of "three conditions" of the soul: attachment, detachment, and indifference. On a hasty glance they may bear a shallow resemblance to each other. Such souls, if we do not know them truly, may all appear to be satisfied. But the difference among the three is profound. *Attachment* is that state of the soul so mercilessly scoured already and repeatedly in the *Quartets*, namely, "appetency", or "the fear of fear". One clings desperately to *things*, which will abandon us as we fall into the "Dark". Then there is *detachment*: the saint who has let the darkness come upon him, and who is free from these fatuous attachments, and straining forward to the dance. And "growing between them" this *indifference*. With this one, you can't tell from the

outside whether the man is satisfied because, as with attachment, he seems at peace by virtue of having every*thing* that
he wants or satisfied because he has embraced the dark and
has forsworn his attachment to baubles. But the truth of the
matter is that indifference ". . . resembles the others as death
resembles life". Ah. How grotesque, and with what quiet
dismissal Eliot has treated it. It is sterile, in a limbo between
"The live and the dead nettle". Nettles sting. Sooner or later,
your attachment to things will sting you, most notably when
it pulls itself from your grasp. And certainly the saints will
tell us of the sting involved in true detachment. One lets
go of one's best loves and of one's fondest pleasures, not
through masochism, but in the interest of lasting freedom
and bliss. But indifference: it is an *ersatz* tranquillity of soul;
it is the threshold of hell, since what I have done in this case
is to shut down self-scrutiny and memory and all the other
faculties by which I might undertake to fare forward and
have spun a cocoon of pure cynicism around me, which,
alas, is the very avatar of hell.

But, with no pause, continuing straight on from these
nettles, we find ourselves hailed with "This is the use of
memory: for liberation. . . ."

Memory is the faculty par excellence of repentance and
recovery. One undertakes "the rending pain of re-enactment /
Of all that you have done, and been". Right. I will rip up
the veneer of these fatuous attachments; and I will break
through this integument of indifference with which I have
shielded myself from the daunting truth; and I will descend
lower, into the darkness, which shall be the darkness of God.
Detachment.

A foolish onlooker will shout "Puritanism!" "Denial of
life!" "Masochism!" No. The whole thing moves toward "not
less of love but expanding / Of love beyond desire, and so

liberation / From the future as well as the past". How can we not hear the first lines of "Burnt Norton" ringing? It is this dismal sequence of *mere* past, present, and future that drains everything, including ourselves, away. So—where is that everlasting present which, in this mortal life, is so bedeviled by past and future? At the Still Point.

These loves, which are so familiar to us all—patriotism, for example: it is good, so far as it goes, but of course it concerns itself with the ephemeral, which history drains away. To be trapped inside of history or to make it into some ultimate, as Engels and Marx did, is to invite servitude (we need only look at Stalin's Russia or Mao's China to see what happens to us mortals when history is deified: talk about servitude . . .). On the other hand, "History may be freedom", insofar as I bring it into the service of my own penitential raking through of the past, learning from my own ghastly missteps and those of all men since the beginning. All of that vanishes, along with the self that loved it all, as much as it could.

"To become renewed, transfigured, in another pattern".

How so? Well, one learns, or *may* learn, from sin. We all know that, even though to say so sounds perilous insofar as it would seem to be a warrant for more sin. But Saint Augustine's "*O felix culpa Adae!*" (O happy fault of Adam) was not blasphemy, nor any invitation to the bacchanale. The fault of Adam (and of all of us) was trumped by Grace. It brought about the Incarnation. *Et homo factus est.* And was made man. We all kneel during the liturgy at these insupportable words.

And again we find the Lady Julian of Norwich. "Sin is Behovely." She was on Saint Augustine's side. Of course I cannot say to myself, "Oh! Sin behooves me, eh? Right. Here we go!" But from the point of view of Redemption (which is only rightly seen from the Still Point), we may see that the worst thing was transfigured in another pattern. Our sin ruined our innocence, but it brought about our crowning with the life of God himself (it is called Beatitude).

The next two lines sound unforgivably silly. All shall be well, is it! You sound like a spring lamb frolicking in a meadow. Poor thing: What does he know of the knife that will cut his throat?

No. The Lady Julian, and the *Quartets*, arrive at this astonishing place *only after having canvassed the whole breadth and depth of horror.*

In the next twenty-three lines, the poet reflects on this place (Little Gidding, that is). He thinks of all the sorts and conditions of men who have been here—many of them on opposite sides of (no doubt) the English Civil War. One was a king, and some had been hanged—either by the king or by his foe Oliver Cromwell, although we cannot think of three men on a scaffold without also remembering Calvary. Some were obscure. One died "blind and quiet". Milton? It does not really matter.

Our recalling of this great company of the dead who have come here is no sentimental attempt to turn time back; nor is it "an incantation" to override time by summoning up the White Rose of York or the Red Rose of Lancaster (a war preceding the Civil War by two hundred years) in the interest of redoing it all and getting it right. Nor is it an attempt to peer into the Celestial Rose: we have no warrant for that yet. What's past is past. The point is, the whole ragtag and bobtail are now "folded in a single party". The dead.

An irony appears. "Whatever we inherit from the fortunate"—any legacies, pedigree, or heirlooms—we have, as it turns out from this perspective of death and the past, "taken from the defeated", whose legacies and possessions were taken over by the fortunate victors. We recall the boarhound and the boar: both participate in the dance. Or Arjuna, who was admonished to carry through his appointed task as avenger, since in the end his role and that of his victim are taken up into the Dance. The fortunate and the defeated, it seems, both constitute part of the choreography.

What, pray, is this "symbol", perfected in death, which the victors and the vanquished seem to have left to us? Surely their combined legacy to us constitutes a symbol of the Dance, which, chaotic as it all appears here under the species of *time*, is "perfected in death", which in turn is the agent bringing us through the scrim of past, present, and future, which can all look tragic, up to the Celestial Rose, where— next lines—"All shall be well and / All manner of thing shall be well. . . ." (It might also be pointed out here that Eliot, being an Anglo-Catholic, would have been familiar with the old usage of the word "symbol", referring to the Creed of the Church. In that usage, the connotation is of an articulating, or a full statement. Readers, if they choose, may see whether this throws any alternative light on the matter.)

And, again, this is not the poet, much less the Lady Julian, papering over tragedy with the rosy tissue of wishful thinking. The following lines belie any such fatuity: "By the purification of the motive / In the ground of our beseeching".

This "ground"—the firm foundation upon which we stand when we send up our supplications, if, say, we are a broken king, or any of us undergoing the ordeals of life in time—this ground is *Thou*. "Thou art the ground of our beseeching", says the Lady Julian in her *Revelations of Divine Love*. Not hope, for hope would be hope for the wrong thing; and not love, for love (at least our little shortsighted loves) would be love of the wrong thing. What we address in our beseechings is the Thou at the Still Point.

This carries our understanding of the Still Point a very

great step forward: when it comes to the world of prayer, which supervenes past, present, and future, we find ourselves addressing, not a theoretical mathematical point, but a Thou. The whole of the *Quartets* has been inveigling us along toward this. And, of course, one stands on this ground only insofar as one's motives have been purified from all hopes and loves of the wrong things. *Fiat mihi*, said the pure Virgin: be it done unto me according to thy word. Not, "Oh—could we work it out this way? Or that?" Just *Fiat mihi*. This is the prayer of the bone on the beach, and of the boar, and, let us hope most earnestly, of the merchant bankers and eminent men of letters as they fall into the dark. It is the prayer that most justly follows hard upon the *Kyrie eleison* that is wrung from us at the moment of calamity.

IV

These lyrics in section IV of each of the *Quartets* echo, and follow upon, each other. "Burnt Norton" brought us via burial to the Still Point. "East Coker" brought us, via the wounded surgeon, to Good Friday—certainly the point of intersection par excellence of the timeless with time. "The Dry Salvages" appeals to our Lady to pray for sailors, be they still working or drowned, and for their wives or widows, and brings us to the angelus, which prays the only prayer possible at that intersection, namely, *Fiat mihi*. Now we find the dove again.

Who can it be but the Holy Spirit, who arrives with the terrible flaming tongues that announce "The one discharge from sin and error", namely, the apostolic news of the dripping blood and bloody flesh. If this seems farfetched to any reader not wholly at home in Catholic doctrine, let us put it baldly: that blood and flesh, riven and poured out at Calvary, is believed to be God's offering to us of the forgiveness of sins. Not the huddling into a closet of those sins, nor a sweeping under the rug, nor a papering over: those tactics might appear to appease, briefly. But forgiveness is the only door to reconciliation between us, who live on the unhappy earth endowed by the ruined millionaire, and the Most High, from whom we have fled.

Our only *hope* at this calamitous point lies in our choice of the fire of God's Love, signaled in those incandescent tongues. If we choose despair, we may opt for hell's pyre instead. We can be redeemed from hellfire only by choosing the purification of the divine fire.

If we may speak of any given line(s) as more memorable than any other line(s) in the *Quartets*, I myself would volunteer this next stanza. I am aware that this would not especially please Eliot, who was not dotting this work with "memorable" lines.

How can it be that Love "devised the torment"? It is sadism that does that sort of thing. Well, not in these precincts. There is no purification without fire. Gold testifies to that, and so do the martyrs and other saints. By this time none of us need ask whose Name this unfamiliar Name is. His hands, bleeding like the surgeon's, wove the shirt of flame we cannot shuck off. In Greek myth, such a shirt shows up in the tales of both Medea and Hercules, in both cases a shirt prepared in hate. This shirt is woven by Love. We wear it right to the gates of Beatitude.

So. In the first stanza above, we had a choice of pyres. Here we come to the flat statement of simple fact: we are going to be consumed by fire in any event. That much is patent. The dread dignity with which we mortals are crowned, namely, the dignity of freedom, places the calamitous choice in our

hands. The white and blissful heat of Beatitude or the sul-
phurous inferno of hell.

A parenthetical note: it is the mark of Eliot's identity as a
modern poet that in these *Quartets*, which have no theme other
than the unabashed Catholic notion of salvation, the words
"God", "Christ", "Calvary", and "Gospel" never once occur.
It is not fastidiousness or timorousness that asks this reticence
from Eliot: it is, rather, the imperious demand laid upon the
modern poet that he contrive to speak of this theme in words
that will quietly steal a march on the unbelieving modern
reader without ever once betraying the strategy or falling into
any periphrastic study in a worn-out poetical fashion. Those
loaded words belong to the apostolic world. May heaven
forbid that the *poet* borrow from that vocabulary—most noble
in itself, but unavailable to the modern poet, whose task it is
to triumph in the intolerable wrestle with words and meaning. He can't do that with borrowed words.

V

The fifth movement brings us full circle. The foregoing four
books have, each in its way, concerned themselves with the
beginning and the end and with the paradox that each is
contained in the other. Time present and time past are both
perhaps present in time future. At the Still Point of the turning world. The Dance. Reconciliation and not appeasement.

So here. The first two lines repeat the theme. The acorn,
which would seem to be a beginning, already has its end in
itself: oakness. And, as Mary, Queen of Scots, knew, to make
an end on the chopping block is to arrive at the true beginning. The end (Paradise) is where we started from (Eden,
otherwise known as Paradise).

For the poet, every phrase and sentence that he gets right is both an end ("Aha! At last! I've finally got the line right") and a beginning, since words slip, slide, and perish, and he must be forever faring forward in his art.

We find a long parenthesis here, where the poet speaks of his materials (words, which move in time, we will recall). The great thing is to get the word in the place where it will do its work of supporting the others. Poetry is not a matter of regaling us with astounding words that trumpet away in their own interest. And it must be the *right* word, falling into neither the ditch of diffidence (an evading of *le mot juste* through awkwardness) nor that of ostentation ("Oh-ho! There's a word for you!"—although some wag among us might want to murmur, "What about 'haruspicate', dear Eliot?"). The poet's argot must evince "An easy commerce of the old and the new": if you need a Shakespearean word, so be it; but it must not muscle aside the line that has a modern flavor about it. And so forth. These lines are smooth sailing even for the first-time reader. The parenthesis ends by evoking the midnight peasant dance, the "dignified and commodiois [sic] sacrament . . . which betokeneth concorde".

If we listened to Dante's discourse on that morning after the blitz, we will agree that "Every poem [is] an epitaph." *Hic jacet.* Here lies my poem. Last year's words belong to last year. The full pail is empty. Likewise any action—even our virtues, we will recall—is a step to the guillotine, or the stake, or the deep. Certainly it is a step toward the time when my very tombstone will have weathered away to illegibility.

And that (death, in case we were in any doubt, this late in the game) is where we start. In our end is our beginning. Our very birth is a birth among the dead, since both we and our parents "are" dead, from the vantage point of the future, which is contained in time past. Or these dead return, in the conjunction of future and past, and we find ourselves on stage in the present, as it were.

"The moment of the rose [youth, beauty, spring] and the moment of the yew-tree" in the churchyard whose fingers reach down and clutch at our skulls in their coffins are "of equal duration". At the Still Point, the long line of time is compressed into this infinitesimal dot. Duration is inoperative here.

If you ("a people") deny, or seek to erase, your history in the interest of upstaging it with some supposititious "present" (as, for example, when some superannuated movie queen resorts to face-lift after face-lift, or when the Russian Revolution seeks to begin history in 1917), you have gained nothing. You haven't effected what you hoped, namely, escape from time. You aren't thereby redeemed from time. Time ticks on, wrinkles, tsars, and all. You are stuck with your history. And since "history is a pattern / Of timeless moments", why try to elude it anyway? All you have are timeless moments. Each one is yet another intersection, where you are given the chance to descry the timeless—the Still Point, that is. If you insist on sweeping it all away, you are a fool.

So, here in the draughty church at smokefall, or in the church at East Coker, or here in the secluded chapel at Little Gidding, we may say that "History is now and England." All time, past, present, or future, and all place, since we have started from anywhere, from the place we would be likely to come from, happen to be, effectively, *now*, and *in England*, since that is the (unimportant, but supremely important) time and place in which we find ourselves, and which, by the by, is the only time and place ever offered to us, and which is the point of intersection.

Eliot floats the next line in a sort of space that may be

understood to conclude the foregoing lines or else to prepare us for the very last lines. There is no punctuation.

This line gathers up all that has gone before in the *Quartets*. From the opening lines of "Burnt Norton" right on through, we have been drawn by "this Love and the voice of this Calling". The capital letters tell their own story. The poet remains faithful to the canons that have governed his words throughout: we will fare forward, inexorably, toward the Still Point; but we will not lapse into the peddling argot of theology. What an untutored reader might suppose to be circuitousness or timidity on Eliot's part turns out to be the most remorselessly direct line to where we are going. It is called poetry, not map reading.

Or, we may (indeed, we cannot avoid it) connect that unpunctuated line with the following, and final, lines of the whole thing. With that drawing, and the call of that voice, "We shall not cease from exploration." Fare forward, travelers. We have come this way, taking the route we would be likely to take from the place we are likely to have come from, taking any route, actually, and we find that it is the same— now, and in England, or at whatever intersection of the timeless with time we happen to find ourselves.

But what do we find? Ah. We have arrived where we started, and lo—we recognize the place for the first time. How so? Because before we had been awakened by these *Quartets*, we were shuffling along in more or less of a torpor, not really recognizing anything particular. Just the quotidian routines. This subway is halting too long here. I have nothing to think about. My feelings are an imprecise mess anyway. Don't talk to me about old age—I'll face that much later. I don't want to belong to another. I shall protect myself with the carapace of indifference, thank you very much.

Four Quartets, like an archangelic horn, has blown all of

that to smithereens. We are here. The place where we *all* started, of course, is Eden, otherwise known as Paradise. It has taken how many eons for us to circle through the *selv' oscura* and arrive here? Here is the gate, unknown but, oddly, remembered, like some fugitive glance from our infancy that we cannot quite conjure and yet find ourselves remembering, oh, so dimly. And, ironically, "the last of earth left to discover / Is that which was the beginning". Again, how so? Well, our circumnavigations and peregrinations and evadings and detourings have all, somehow, missed the place. Somehow, we blundered right on past Eden in our haste to get on to the next spa. But it has been here since the beginning. We needn't have gone any farther than Little Gidding, or East Coker, or our own sitting room, for that matter.

All those fleeting moments that pierced us with *sehnsucht*: Shall we follow this river all the way to its unexplored source? Hark! Is that a waterfall there *au fond du bois*? The children playing in the apple tree in that story: Will I ever glimpse such innocent merriment? Well, what is one to do with such lance-like impressions anyway? One can never really *know* them, surely, since grown-ups don't spend their time looking for fantasies. Nevertheless, I cannot escape the notion that I *have* heard those sounds, or at least half heard them, in the stillness. The trouble with the whole business, however, is that it is as unstable and elusive as the space between two waves of the sea. How much significance do you want me to attach to these undulations of my fancy?

Quite a bit, suggests the poet. But you must be quick. Now. Here. Now. Always. The point of intersection, that Still Point of which those "fancies" are the merest glimpses, is here, now, and always. Every moment opens out onto that vista.

But there is a daunting condition. You must, through prayer, observance, discipline, thought, and action, have reached "A condition of complete simplicity".

Oh. Well, that shouldn't be too hard. I'll just pause here and get quiet for a minute, and presto! Simplicity.

Not quite. The thing about this condition is that it *costs*. Every farthing you have. It will ask of you "not less than everything".

Oh.

At the far—the very far—end of all our exploring, in which there are no shortcuts, "All shall be well and / All manner of thing shall be well. . . ." The children in the apple tree. The source of the longest river. The hidden waterfall. Through the first gate into our first world. The water rising out of sunlight, and the lotos rising with it. Beyond the wave cry and the wind cry and the vast waters and the cry of the petrel and the porpoise.

"When the tongues of flame are in-folded / Into the crowned knot of fire / And the fire and the rose are one."

Here at the Still Point, where the fire and the rose are one, the smallest commentary seems a sacrilege, like verifying, or informing curiosity, or carrying report. We are here to kneel. But because, alas, my book is not the poem, I must finish my job. All the flames, whether from the dark dove descending the air, or of the suffering allotted to our mortality, or of purgation and purifying (they may all be the same), are here gathered into this "crowned knot", like the crest at the top of a coat of arms. Here are victory, bliss, and nobility after our long apprenticeship. And here the fire that refines, not without pain, and the rose, blooming with everlasting youth, beauty, fragrance, and perfection, are one.